The Barber's Conundrum and Other Stories

Observations on Life from the Cheap Seats

JOHN HARTNETT

EARLYBIRD PUBLISHING

ISBN-13: 978-0615741154

*Cover photograph by Jack Delano, May1941, Farm Security Administration -
Office of War Information Photograph Collection (Library of Congress)*

Book design by John Hartnett

DEDICATION

For Jeanne, Jack, Annabelle and Caroline

CONTENTS

INTRODUCTION

Where do I begin? You've never heard of me, I've never heard of you and yet here we are. Could it be fate? God certainly does move in mysterious ways, particularly if He had anything to do with *The Jersey Shore* running for 66 episodes.

I doubt it's fate.

So who am I to write a book? Nobody, really. Never had my own sitcom or starred in a movie. Never started a chain of sushi bar slash laundromats. Never ran for political office. Nothing notable to speak of with the possible exception that I once went without showering for six weeks but that was when we had an exchange student from Belgium who apparently had some sort of aversion to bathing and I didn't want to make him self conscious. The only time Jens had a bar of soap in his hands during the entire time he stayed with us was when he helped my mother unload the groceries.

Truth be told, I'm just a regular guy, someone like you perhaps. Someone who appreciates the simple things in life. Someone who still takes great pride in mowing his own lawn. My wife happened to be standing over my shoulder when I wrote that last line and said, "Why don't you tell them the truth and that the only reason you mow your own lawn is because you're cheap?"

I live in New Jersey. Married, three kids. You just met my wife. We have a dog named Hartley. No, that's not right. *I* have a dog named Hartley.

Hartley was supposed to be my children's dog ("Please, please? We'll walk it, we'll feed it! What do we have to do to prove it to you?!!!") but make no mistake, it's my dog — an indisputable fact never less in question than at 2 o'clock in the morning when I am the only one in the house who will acknowledge, let alone investigate the source of a high pitched keening wail and what very well could be to someone who has just been jolted awake from the dead of sleep, the desperate howling of a man who has been buried alive and attempting to scratch his way out of a coffin.

"Didn't anyone hear Hartley howling last night and scratching at the back door at two in the morning?"

"What time? No. I must have been out like a light. Do you have $6? They're having a bake sale at school"

So what's in the book? It's a collection of essays I wrote for a newspaper syndicate in NJ and various other observational and satirical short pieces that look at raising children, marriage, school, popular culture and entertainment, politics. Things like that. I wrote these pieces to share a few laughs — there's enough bad news out there — nothing too heavy, nothing too confrontational, nothing too racy. Racy, how often do you get to use that word? Outdated, I know. You're probably picturing me now as one of those 1950's crewcut guys who take off their suit jacket and put on a cardigan sweater when they get home from work.

I can live with that.

Thanks for reading!

John Hartnett

December, 2012

QUIET PLEASE, SOCCER GAME IN PROGRESS

Icy temperatures far below normal. Gale force winds. Stinging sheets of horizontal rain. Cascading rivers of mud. This abnormal change in our spring weather patterns can only mean one thing. Somebody somewhere has scheduled a children's soccer game.

My daughter had two games this weekend. Like every game before them -- it rained. Temperatures never got above 46 degrees unless you were lucky enough to spill coffee in your lap. I saw two four-year old girls selling shots of Sambucca out of the back of their parent's Suburban.

In spite of the inclement weather parents were there in force. This was an end of the season tournament and there were eleven fields, all of them filled with hard charging boys and girls and all of them lined with parents, siblings, spectators, coaches, assistant coaches, and the occasional European trainer, whose ubiquitous cries of "Unlucky!" or "Well done!" in English and Irish accents provided a little extra ambience in a "Tom Brown's School Days" sort of way.

While my daughter warmed up in preparation of warming up for her game, I took a walk along the line of soccer fields, stopping occasionally to watch the games for a moment or two. The ages of the children varied, as did the gender and the level of skill but nonetheless a similar pattern emerged and along with it a revelation. Some adults are just plain nuts.

The screaming, the endless screaming. "Go! To goal, to goal!" "Watch number 3, watch number 3! Nooooooo!! I told you to watch number 3!" "Shoot! Shoot! Now shoot! Now, now, now!" "Take it up the side! The side, keep going, keep going!" "Sarah's in the middle, she's in the middle! The middle, the middle! PASS! PASS!" "Ohhhhhhh!!!!"

I stood mesmerized by a coach who stalked along the sidelines shouting detailed instructions to his players as if he were a human joystick that could control their physical movements with just the sound of his voice. "Danny, move left." "Dribble right and go, right and go!" "Take it left and cross. Cross! Aahh, for God's sake! I said cross!"

Note to all parents and coaches who scream from the sidelines: Your kids can't hear a word you say. Want to control your players' every move? Get a foosball table. As much as you want your kids to score, there are kids on the other team who don't want them to score. I'm surprised parents haven't tried screaming at the kids on the opposing team. "Hey number 11, stand still and do nothing!"

I heard a mother offer the following words of encouragement to her daughter as she waited for the second half to begin, "Do it up right. Make me proud." Do it up right? I was tempted to alert the referee, "Mangled syntax on the field. Everyone take a knee."

Can you imagine how parents who shout at their kids at soccer games would fare if they were subjected to the same treatment at work? Say they're in the process of admitting an emergency room patient while the boss watches from across the room. "Not the injury, the insurance card, check the insurance card first! We don't take United Health anymore. Oxford, yes! Oxford! Quick, the copy machine's free, the machine's free. Hurry! Someone's coming with a huge file, run! Run! Keep going! Oooooh!"

Years ago, I used to play little league baseball. Most game days, I slid my glove on the handlebars of my bike and rode over to the field by myself. My teammates did the same thing. Our parents came to watch if they had the time, if they were busy, they didn't. Sometimes we won, sometimes we lost. Sometimes I got a couple of hits and caught a couple of balls and sometimes I didn't. Big deal. It was summertime.

After the game, I'd ride back, put my bike in the garage and walk in the house. My father would ask me how we did, I'd tell him a little bit about how the game went and that would be it.

Two minutes of conversation at best --and in my mind-- still the perfect length of time to spend discussing any game between a bunch of nine-year-old kids.

THERE BUT FOR THE GRACE OF GOD GOES THE WEATHER REPORTER

Announcer: NNN's Never Ending News Network continues with its award winning, trademark pending, never ending coverage of Hurricane Edna.

Anchorwoman Lindsay Brockport: Welcome back to NNN. Hurricane Edna continues to batter the Florida Keys with 165 mile per hour winds. More than 16 inches of rain has fallen in the past hour and waves have been measured as high as 75 feet. Thankfully, all islands in the Keys have been evacuated, with the exception of several disaster relief teams who are stationed in specially constructed steel bunkers designed to withstand even the most severe hurricane conditions. This is truly a storm for the record books and if you were unfortunate enough to still be on one of the Florida Keys, a bunker 35 feet underground is the only place you'd have a chance. Bill Tremaine, from sister station KKW in Miami is standing by in Key Largo.

Bill Tremain: Good afternoon, Lindsay. I'm standing just a hundred yards outside of the disaster relief bunker in Key Largo. A moment ago I was standing five yards outside the disaster relief bunker but as anyone who has seen, read or heard anything about hurricanes knows – this is what happens when you venture out into 165 mile and hour winds -- you get tossed around like a beach ball at a Jimmy Buffet concert. The rain has really started to pick up as have surf conditions and if I can ask my cameraman Tom to zoom out a bit here, you can see that flooding has started to become a factor as the water is now an inch or two above my …waist. (Suddenly desperate, he jams his hand into his pocket and retrieves a rectangular object that when turned over releases a ten second stream of water.) There goes a $499 Iphone.

Lindsay: Dire conditions indeed, Bill. Was that a car and what appeared to be the roofs of several houses flying overhead?

Bill: Yes it was and to reiterate for those of you who have never seen, read or heard anything about hurricanes, this is typical hurricane behavior. Torrential rains cause flooding, and gale force winds cause very heavy objects to become briefly airborne until they reestablish themselves in places where they are generally not wanted or (nervously scanning the sky) in some unfortunate situations – not expected. In fact, Lindsay, experts strongly recommend against being outside in a hurricane. People get hurt in them, say people like Tom and me here.

Lindsay: How have you managed to remain stationary while much heavier objects like trailers and cows soar just inches over your head?

Bill: Sigrid Olsen, my producer, risked her own safety and what is certain to be the irreversible shrinking of her pants suit to lash my legs to this palm tree with a pair of bungee cords. That's Sigrid behind me about to reenter the bunker. (With her back turned, she waves halfheartedly and quickly disappears behind the steel door.) God bless her.

Lindsay: What can you tell us about the residents of Key Largo?

Bill: Judging by the fact that they're gone, I'd say they possess higher than average intelligence. It's unlikely you'd find a reporter in the bunch. You may have noticed while we were talking that the rain is now starting to come in horizontally which as you know is quite different than vertical rain.

Lindsay: Yes, and for the sake of our viewers who are wondering about the distinction, vertical rain falls upon the region of the skull where hair is most commonly found while horizontal rain falls upon one's face, usually hitting the nose first before landing upon the other areas. Vertical rain is more dangerous of course, particularly for those who wear glasses to see objects more clearly or for those who are in the habit of eating with their mouths open. Bill, what should people do if exposed to horizontal rain?

Bill: Experts recommend wiping your glasses off from time to time with a terry cloth towel or soft cotton t-shirt to avoid scratching the lenses. For people who eat or sleep with their mouths open, it's best to stay indoors until precipitation forecasts drop to below fifteen percent. I'm noticing now that the water has risen up to my chin, Lindsay. Tom and I had better start making our way to higher ground.

Lindsay: Good idea, it is starting to look a little treacherous out there. Final thoughts before we wrap up?

Bill: While we were talking I was thinking about the lyrics to that Petula Clark song, "Don't sleep in the subway darling. Don't stand in the pouring rain."

Lindsay: And…?

Bill: Do you think she was dating a reporter when she wrote that?

THE BARBER'S CONUNDRUM

I now hold the record for the longest consecutive streak of bad haircuts since the invention of the sheep shears in 1,000 BC. Since the age of 3, I have experienced 378 bad haircuts in a row, and have the 379th scheduled for next week, God willing.

I blame no one but myself. I am cursed with wavy hair and cowlicks --a combination so volatile and unpredictable, I actually carry a doctor's prescription for a hat.

If I wore a crew cut, this piece wouldn't be necessary. It's not a look that works for me. I tried one when I was 23. Fifteen minutes after I walked out of the barbershop, I was standing in a police lineup accused of robbing a string of gas stations in Oklahoma.

I have to keep my hair a little longer to avoid the career criminal look but short enough so people don't assume I work clown parties on the weekends.

I'm a barber's worst nightmare because I'm not a crew cut guy. They enjoy giving crew cuts because all they need is a pair of clippers and a little conversation. There's no finesse in crew cuts, no risks. Whenever I sink into the chair, they automatically reach for the clippers and when I tell them I just want a trim, they start looking at my head like it's the Manhattan Project. It's not uncommon to have three barbers looking at my head at the same time, like baseball managers standing around the pitcher's mound deciding whether to try a little pep talk or send for the reliever. I've had barbers spontaneously retire while I sat in their chairs. One even tried to convince me that I'd be better off cutting it myself.

My quest for a decent haircut has taken me around the country. I've tried barbers and hairdressers in hotels, airports, in vacation cities – even at a barber college where the cuts are free because the kids are in training. I figured a barber college would be an excellent place to get a good, well-executed haircut because the kids would be so excited about entering a new profession.

I scheduled an appointment at a local college and the dean assigned me to a young woman named Ingrid who was actually the class valedictorian. She truly was an artist. Half way through my haircut, which was looking spectacular, she received a letter from the board of regents notifying her that her graduate thesis on the benefits of washing a customer's hair after a haircut to remove the excess clippings would not be published. She ran out of the salon in tears followed by her concerned classmates and I found myself walking home with half the best haircut I ever had in my life. Believe me, I was tempted to keep it that way.

I've done some duplicitous things in search of a decent haircut. Even lying. Whenever I sit down in the chair of a new barber or hairdresser, the first thing out of my mouth is, "I'm getting married this Saturday, and I really need this haircut to look good." Once I made the mistake of using the same marriage line on a barber I had been to before. He looked at me coldly and said, "I thought you told me you were getting married last year."

"I did," I said. "But when my fiancé took one look at the haircut you gave me a year ago, she called the whole thing off."

With all the technology that is available, I don't know why I can't get a decent haircut. It seems like those Lasik machines they use to correct vision would work if they made a couple of adjustments. You probably wouldn't have to do much more than mount one inside a helmet type device. I don't know that I'd trust a barber to use one of those but if you were a licensed eye doctor looking for a competitive edge you could offer corrective eye surgery and a haircut for one, all inclusive price.

In my experience, getting a good haircut isn't a matter of price either. I've paid as little as $8 and as much as $75 for bad haircuts, and the only difference between the inexpensive salons and the expensive ones is that sometimes you can get a glass of organic juice.

The average scalp has 100,000 hairs. Approximately 50,000 of mine grow in different directions. Maybe what I need is a comb made from the bone of an old sheepdog.

THE ONLY CHILD REARING BOOK A PARENT WILL EVER NEED

Introducing The Only Child Rearing Book a Parent Will Ever Need!

Are you a parent? Potential parent? Expecting parent? Do you ever read parenting books just to celebrate the fact that you aren't a parent and still have your freedom? If so, you're going to love my new book, *Kids You Can Count On*.

Kids You Can Count On is guaranteed to help you raise perfect children effortlessly. How can I make such a statement without biting my bottom lip until blood comes out? Simple! Every technique I used to raise my three beloved kids to become bright, happy, polite, and well-adjusted is not in the book. Why? Because none of the techniques worked. My kids' behavior had me drinking Maalox out of industrial sized containers -- but the important thing is now I know what went wrong! Now I get it! And that's what's in the book. Why suffer years of frustration raising kids through trial and error, when I've already done the suffering for you?

Here are some sample insights and real life examples from the book, guaranteed to save you time, reduce stress and most importantly --raise the type of child you'd admit was yours even if you weren't being interrogated by the police!

What I Learned About Teaching Respect for Adults:

Never let your child call an adult by their first name. Why? Because right from the beginning a child who refers to you by your first name believes she is your equal, two days later she's convinced she's your superior and four days later, you're convinced she's your superior. Here's an excerpt from a conversation between my 44-year old babysitter, Katherine, and my three-year old daughter Annie, who had been encouraged to call Katherine by her first name.

Katherine: Annie, honey, it's time for your nap.

Annie: I'm not sleepy, Kathy, but thanks for your concern. Would you be a dear and get me another juice box?

How to fix it so your kid never calls anyone by their first name again? See page 43!

The Right Way to Communicate with Your Child:

Military philosophy may be "Don't ask. Don't tell," but for parents and kids it should be "Don't ask. Tell!" What happens when you stop giving your kids choices? You get your life back, that's what! Here's an excerpt from a school day breakfast discussion between my children and my wife -- before we knew any better:

Mother: What would you like for breakfast?

Annie: Bacon and eggs.

Jim: Pancakes with sausage.

Cathy: Oatmeal.

Mother: There's no time. You all took thirty-minute showers. How about cereal or toast?

Annie: I want bacon and eggs.

Jim: If we're not having pancakes then I don't want anything.

Cathy: Cereal *and* toast!

Mother: Let me see what I can do.

A smart lawyer never asks a question in a courtroom without already knowing the answer. Conversations with children should be handled no differently. Here's an excerpt from a school day breakfast discussion between my wife and children after she read Chapter 6, *How to Say "I'm Only Saying This Once" and Mean It.*:

Mother: What would you like for breakfast this morning? I'll give you a hint. It's corn flakes and you have ten minutes to finish eating.

Need a handy reference for replacing common open ended questions with time saving imperative sentences? Look no further than page 119!

Television: Friend or Foe?

For years we let our kids watch television whenever they wanted until one day, my wife and I tripped down a flight of stairs together, sustaining coma-inducing injuries. While we lay in a tangled heap on the floor, our children watched television until the power company turned off the electricity. Our lifeless bodies were finally discovered by our panic stricken children, who in spite of their harrowing ordeal had the presence of mind to call our neighbors and ask politely if they could watch TV at their house.

Don't wait for a coma to get the wakeup call that your kids are spending way too much time in front of the television.

Tv troubles in your home? Consult Chapter 9, From Couch Potatoes to Planting Potatoes, includes simple two-step program for turning off the television and turning on your kids ...to the simple pleasures of back breaking yard work!

How to Slay the Birthday Party Goliath

I realized our children's birthday parties were getting out of line when one of the tigers, I can't remember now whether it was Siegfried's or Roy's, pounced on my mother-in-law during our daughter Cathy's first birthday celebration. Luckily Cathy wasn't traumatized by the event since she didn't wake up from her nap until fifteen minutes after 224 of her closest friends and relatives headed for home. While there is no such thing as debtor's prison anymore, my wife and I were so deeply in hock from charging our children's birthday bashes that the state legislature briefly discussed opening a local debtor's prison just for us. *Kids You Can Count On* shows you how to say adios to $10,000 birthday party singalongs with Willie Nelson and hello to $30 pizza parties!

Can't make smores without flying Emeril Lagasse in for the weekend? Turn to Appendix II, Simple Dishes Even You Can Cook.

Testimonials Keep Pouring In!

Here's what parents who've read *Kids You Can Count On* have to say about my book:

"Since using the techniques outlined in your book, my children's behavior has improved so much friends stop them on the street to ask if they've been adopted." -- Terry K, Orlando, FL.

"My wife and I have adapted your time saving 'Don't ask. Tell!' philosophy and the resulting peace and quiet has been so rewarding, we've taken the philosophy one step further by requiring our children to submit all questions to us in writing. Who would believe a home with five children could be more tranquil than a monastery?" -- Eddie Jondo, Lincoln, NE

The Offer You'd Be a Fool to Pass Up!

I'm so convinced that *Kids You Can Count On* is the only book you'll need to keep your kids in line, I've raised the price from $29.99 to $39.99. Order today and I'll even throw in my award winning pamphlet for kids, "You're the Reason Why Santa Isn't Coming This Year." Operators are standing by...

CONFESSIONS OF AN ARMCHAIR THRILL SEEKER

I subscribe to "Outside", a magazine that celebrates the lives of those who live life to its fullest: mountain climbers, surfers, explorers, white water rafters, back packers, triathletes, people who live for the opportunity to test the limits of their physical and psychological endurance, people who thrive on being dropped into completely foreign environments, people who have come face to face with death and lived to tell the tale.

In other words, people like me.

Forget it, I can't even write with a straight face. I haven't had an outdoor adventure since the day I took the family to Hershey Park and forgot where I parked the car.

I used to be an outdoor guy, used to love backpacking in the middle of nowhere and then one day I literally, completely lost interest while in the middle of a trip. My brother and I were in California scrambling up the exposed face of some mountain in the Sierras with 40 pound packs strapped to our backs. It was a typical, exhilarating high altitude backpacking environment: gale force winds so strong and relentless you could die and not fall down, a temperature of 26 degrees, and an eclectic mix of snow, sleet and freezing rain.

As we sat huddled against a rock to wait out the weather like we'd done a dozen times before, I turned to my brother and shouted to be heard above the sound of my own chattering teeth and the howling wind. "I no longer find this enjoyable," I said, although I didn't use those exact words.

And that was it, my brain shut off the chemicals triggering the desire to wear goose down vests and suspend food between trees to avoid meeting bears and released the one's triggering the desire to subscribe to magazines about people who wear goose down vests and suspend food between trees to avoid meeting bears.

That day, my brother graciously agreed to hike back down to where it was 75 degrees and sunny and we made camp at a little log cabin themed motel offering free HBO which was conveniently located next to a pristine watering hole offering plenty of game, fresh water and a pool table.

Yes, I had come down from the mountain a wiser man. It was there in the smoky haze of Hector's Hideway that I realized that there are character building challenges associated with any recreational activity and one need not stagger and crawl 12,000 feet up the side of a rock during a blizzard to test one's fortitude, you can do the same thing playing a game of straight pool for money against a mood swinging 280 pound motorcycle mechanic named Shugs who brings his own cue stick, enjoys showing strangers his wanted posters and makes strangling gestures with his hands while you're lining up a shot.

These days, the occasion to play pool with psychologically fragile fugitives from the law in backwater dives doesn't present itself as often as you'd expect so I continue to seek out other challenges closer to home.

On weekends, just attempting to get out of bed quietly without waking the children in order to read the paper in peace is a major challenge that offers a great sense of achievement whenever I can make it to the Metro section before being besieged with relentless, repeated requests from my eleven-year old daughter to make her breakfast.

Another challenge is of course the selection of the fastest checkout line in the supermarket, a feat that requires a vast array of skills and experience combining the assessment of shopper behavior (cash vs. check, self bagging vs. the delegation of bagging, possession of a store discount card vs. the often fictionalized "my spouse has the store discount card"), the knowledge of products (quickly identifying those items most likely to require a price check), the assessment of the mental acuity and physical dexterity of the cashier and the raw physical stamina and speed required to beat another shopper who covets the same position in line.

I also enjoy the red light green light challenge, in which the car in front of you moves so slowly you are tempted to leap out of your car and run past the offending vehicle just so you can shake your fist at the driver. The challenge comes when the car, moving at a snail's pace, approaches a traffic light. As the light turns amber, the driver suddenly becomes possessed by the spirit of Mario Andretti and soars through the intersection as if shot from a cannon. It is here, like many of those celebrated in "Outside Magazine" where you have the opportunity to test both your physical and psychological endurance. Physical -- by riding the rear bumper of the car in front of you and sailing through the light right behind them as if one long vehicle, psychologically -- by letting the source of your frustration go and waiting patiently for the next green light.

Yes, these are the humble challenges in my life now. No more rock climbing, white water rafting, introducing square dancing to headhunters in New Guinea. And yet, the hope remains that one day there might be a magazine about guys like me. They could call it "Inside".

HOW BANANAS ALMOST DESTROYED MY MARRIAGE

Saturday night my son opened the freezer door, a frozen banana fell out, smashed him on the toe and then my daughter bumped her head on the freezer door when she stood up quickly after retrieving the banana from the floor.

I submit to you that there is no greater window into the complicated dance that is marriage than deconstructing that small, relatively insignificant event.

In the 20 years and 313 days that I have been married to my wife, she has taken hundreds of overripe bananas and stored them in our freezers with the intention of someday making bread out of them. Sadly that day has never come.

I will admit that I am partly to blame, because when the opportunity to be alone in the kitchen presents itself – I surreptitiously remove the frozen bananas and bury them in the garbage. For you see, I was raised to believe that neither fruit or for that matter, deceased ball players such as Ted Williams, should be placed in a freezer once they are past their prime.

Conversely, my wife, who came from a very large family, was raised to believe that overripe fruit should be frozen, not wasted. Her mother taught her to do this, albeit a woman who also stored bananas for decades and never made anything out of them – although legend has it that one was once used as an emergency blackjack during a family function that went awry.

Which one of us is right? Aha! All couples on the dance floor, please.

In the pursuit of marital bliss, one must learn to suppress opinions pertaining to a spouse's adherence to particular practices, beliefs or traditions – no matter how ridiculous you think they may be.

Why? Why shouldn't two people who love and trust each other share their true feelings about such matters? A dumb question, but since I asked it -- I'll answer it just this once. Because for every one silly or irritating habit or idiosyncrasy you can attribute to your spouse – your spouse can come up with two to attribute to you. It's like the arms race and money spent on defense is money not spent on books, a habit of mine my wife believes borders on obsession – although of course she's never said it to my face. Still, a man can sense these things… but so what? That's a whole lot better than actually being confronted with it!

I will admit that very early in our marriage, when I was still naïve, I poked fun at my wife's rationale for freezing mushy bananas rather than tossing them out. Her ice cold, steely eyed response? "I don't like to waste food, and I'm going to make banana bread with them." I never mentioned it again.

Since that time, I will state under oath that not once in our 20 years and 313 days together has my wife walked into the kitchen, opened the freezer door and yelled, "What the heck happened to the bananas I had in the freezer? I was going to make bread today!"

Now I can understand that. I've been "researching" colors to paint our house for six years now and haven't even begun to narrow down the range of possibilities contained within the classification of "off white". It isn't easy --the color of your house tells people a lot about who you are. Right now, it's telling them that I'm lazy but I can live with that.

As we attempted to console our injured children who were howling and hopping about the room in an unintentional homage to the Three Stooges, I have to admit that I was a little perturbed that a frozen banana, of a certain age, (a phrase used to gracefully describe people who are ancient), had been the source of the commotion. I said to my wife, "What is it with you and this obsession with freezing bananas?"

But not out loud, of course.

Instead I said, "We have to find a better spot to store those bananas so they don't fall out like that again."

She searched my face for signs of sarcasm and when there were none to be found, she smiled and set about placing the bananas in a Tupperware container.

With calm restored and the pain of injuries subsiding, I announced that I was going to take a drive over to the bookstore and have a look around. My wife said, "What is it with you and your obsession with buying all these books you never find time to read?"

She said it out loud. Can you believe that?

WHO NEEDS CABLE?

Last November, my wife and I broke a taboo so morally reprehensible, they've never even discussed it on the "Jerry Springer Show". We cancelled our cable TV.

Believe it or not, it was really an easy decision that didn't require the usual anguish and hand wringing associated with other major family decisions such as whether or not a trip to visit relatives should really count as a vacation.

There were two specific incidents that triggered this sweeping reform of our family lifestyle. The first involved my eleven-year old son. One evening, I walked into the room where he sat cross-legged in front of "SpongeBob SquarePants" and asked him to wash his hands before dinner. No response. I leaned over and playfully poked him in the ribs and in a sing song voice said, "Time for dinner." He stared up at me curiously for just an instant as if I were a cloud passing over the sun and then turned back to the television.

No longer singing or playful I crouched down in front of him, blocking his view of the television and said, "Did you hear me? I said time for dinner. Go and wash your hands." I had his attention then but that didn't prevent him from craning his neck to look at the TV over my shoulder.

"Now!" I screamed. My son, finally shocked into a state of true consciousness, said okay and stood up. He took a couple of steps, and as I watched in amazement, he stopped in his tracks and re-glued his eyes to the television screen again as if it had desperately cried out to him, "Jack. Where are you going? I thought we were friends."

We had a quiet meal that evening. Heavy on the sounds of silverware and scraping plates, light on conversation outside of the unusually polite requests to pass the butter, that sort of thing. While unpleasant for the innocent victims, I find that the occasional dinner overloaded with quiet seething and melodrama functions as a sort of chiropractic adjustment to restore the normal family balance. The kids really sense from the tension that they better shape up and you don't have to worry about losing your voice from screaming. Win/win as they say.

The second incident, which occurred a short time later, did involve screaming, my two-year old daughter and "Caillou", a two-dimensional wolf in sheep's clothing from PBS.

I work out of the house and am responsible for getting the kids up and to school and daycare each morning. Often my youngest daughter is the first ready and she will ask to watch "Caillou" while the other kids get dressed and I prepare breakfast. I had no problem with her request; the show is pleasant enough although I find Caillou's bald and disproportionately large head to be a bit disconcerting as I am convinced that anyone with a head that big would be unable to stand up for more than a moment before toppling over. You have to wonder, if the animators are that sloppy, how crisp can the writing be? Nonetheless, once everyone is seated, the rule is that "Caillou" is to be turned off.

So, on this particular morning, breakfast is ready and as I go over to turn off "Caillou", my formerly even keeled daughter unleashes a temper tantrum so shocking it makes Courtney Love look like Audrey Hepburn.

Torn between calling an exorcist and enlisting in the Merchant Marines, I opted for losing my cool. I scream to the heavens above that we will no longer have television in this house. A moment later, the phone rings and the guy from across the street says, "What about the Final Four?" I unhooked the cable, seized the 32 inch TV in a bear hug and stagger to the basement, re-emerging moments later covered in sweat and with my heart thumping so fast, you could see it through my shirt.

"That's that," I announce, grinning maniacally about the room. "The only box you'll be staring at from now on is the one that houses that overfed rabbit at the Library."

A week later the television was back in place.

But we didn't cave in all the way, I swear. First, we only use the television now for DVDs, mainly Friday night --which has become family movie night. The kids have to ask for permission on any other occasion.

Second, and this came as a complete shock to my wife and I, our kids have not complained. We play more games together, they read prodigiously, a word my daughter Annabelle taught me, and they haven't even asked us to have the cable reinstalled.

My wife, who grew up without TV, is in Heaven. As for me, yes, there are times when I am miserable. It's baseball season and I used to like watching the occasional game whenever one was on and regardless of who was playing. But the benefits outweigh the negatives.

I do not miss the news at all and no longer get headaches deciding whether to watch and listen to the correspondent on CNN or to read the news ticker, and just listen to the correspondent or to read the stock prices, occasionally glance at the correspondent and ignore the news ticker completely since it has become so overused it now carries the same sense of urgency as a Captain Morgan Rum banner flown over a beach crowd in August.

But do you want to know what the real upside is? Once again, I can actually recognize my children just as easily from the front of their heads as the back. Win/win as they say.

PROMOTING THE BENEFITS OF CHILD LABOR

Even though it was quite cold this weekend, I noticed a lot more people braving the chilly winds to work outside in their yards. Maybe it's cabin fever that compels people to all step outside on the same day to retrieve dead branches and old leaves that have been lying there in the open for months or maybe it's the same sort of genetic trigger that forces Greenland seals to wake up one morning and swim en masse to Spitsberg like a sea bearing version of the Stepford Wives.

I was out in the yard Sunday but I left the branches and the leaves exactly where they were. This was more of a scouting assignment then a cleanup operation, for my children, particularly my son Jack, will be tackling the yard work with me this Spring.

I believe my responsibilities as a parent include instilling a strong work ethic in my children. As a member of a family, I believe everyone must make an ongoing contribution to maintain the household and that work precedes reward. My son agrees with me but since he believes his real father is Prince Charles, he doesn't really consider himself part of our family and refuses to do anything until the DNA results come back.

Kids. When I was young, I loved working around the house with my father. We had a lot of laughs. Along with my brothers, we put in fences, painted the house, re-shingled the garage, and tore up the yard and reseeded it each and every year because nothing ever grew. People who believe the Moon landing was a hoax also believe the hoax was staged in our backyard.

Yes, we were a little clueless in the handyman department but we all knew that there was no way my father was going to pay someone to do the work when he had four able-bodied boys with tapeworms haunting his refrigerator. If we could do it ourselves, we did it ourselves. Once my brother came home convinced that he had appendicitis but it cleared up when he saw my father leave the room and come back with a copy of Gray's Anatomy and a plumber's helper.

And that's the tradition I want to pass on to my children. Do it yourself surgery. No, I want my children to understand that working together and doing what needs to be done around the house is what being a family is all about.

Last summer I felt Jack was old enough to start taking on more responsibility around the house and I wanted him to experience the things I experienced working with my father when I was his age. There was one incident in particular that sums up the progress we made.

What follows is a true story. And I don't mean that in a Fox News or MSNBC sort of way.

One Friday night, Jack, my daughter Annabelle and I were sitting on the deck listening to music. They asked me why I liked music so much and I explained that sometimes my memory wasn't very good but when I heard a certain song, it would trigger very vivid recollections of people, places and experiences.

The next morning, I woke Jack up and told him that he and I were going to weed the garden and cut back a row of azalea bushes that apparently had gone native while my back was turned. My son lunged for the door but when I informed him that all the windows and exits were sealed and that the TV remote was encased in a block of ice, he gave up. Ten minutes later we were side by side in the yard, flailing and hacking away at anything that photosynthesized.

We worked for close to six hours in the hot sun and it was back breaking work. Finally everything that had been pulled, sawed or clipped lay in a huge pile in the middle of the yard and we set to the task of hauling it all off to the conservation center.

By the fourth trip to the dump, we were exhausted. I was singing along to a song on the radio and Jack turned to me and said, "Hey Dad. Remember when you told me that music makes you remember places and things that you did a long time ago?"

"Yes."

"I hope that whenever you hear the song you were just singing, you remember the day we worked in the yard together pulling up all those weeds and bushes."

I looked at my son as he stared straight ahead out the window, his face coated with grime and sweat, and my eyes filled with tears. He gets it, I thought to myself. He enjoyed working with his dad today.

And then a split second later he muttered, "Because I am never, ever doing this kind of work again."

This summer I'm painting the house. I'll call you when he's finished.

LONDON CALLING

LONDON, April 4, 2007 (Reuters) — Close circuit cameras are to be fitted with loudspeakers to allow security staff to berate people spotted dropping litter, vandalizing property or fighting, the British government said Wednesday.

Audio transcripts derived from conversations between Constable Thomas Coffey and Constable Edna Borges, the very first team assigned to the new video & audio berating surveillance monitoring program located at Middlesbrough Security Station.

April 5, 2007: 9:33 a.m.

Edna: Here's someone now, Thomas, see the older gentleman in the suit? Looks like he has a drink in his right hand. Let me zoom in a bit. Yes, it appears to be a diet soda. Do we warn him not to toss the can on the ground or must we wait until he actually does toss it on the ground?

Thomas: An ounce of prevention never hurt, Edna. Remind the potential litterer that the rubbish bin's just down the corner, there.

Edna: *(audible microphone click)* EXCUSE ME, SIR? YES, YOU THERE WITH THE CAN OF LIQUID IN YOUR RIGHT HAND. Oh, dear, Thomas! He's fallen to his knees and is clutching his ears.

Thomas: You had the speaker on maximum, Edna. Turn it down a bit.

Edna: How silly of me. *(audible microphone click)* IF YOU'VE FINISHED WITH YOUR DRINK, YOU MAY PLACE IT IN THE RUBBISH BIN LOCATED... I think I've alarmed him, he's running away.

Thomas: And he's dropped his can on the ground as well, although in retrospect, I doubt that was his original intention. Perhaps we should wait for an infraction before addressing anyone.

April 5, 2007: 10:33 a.m.

Thomas: Anything, Edna?

Edna: Quite as a mouse, I'm afraid, Thomas.

April 5, 2007: 11:09 a.m.

Thomas: Anything?

Edna: No.

April 5, 2007: 12:18 p.m.

Thomas: *(audible microphone click)* HER NAME WAS LOLA, SHE WAS A SHOWGIRL. WITH YELLOW FEATHERS IN HER HAIR AND A DRESS CUT DOWN TO THERE. SHE WOULD MERENGUE AND DO THE CHA-CHA

Edna: They're starting to come out of the shops now, Thomas.

Thomas: AT THE COPA, COPACABANA! THE HOTTEST SPOT NORTH OF HAVANA! Any suspicious faces in the crowd?

Edna: No, doesn't appear to be.

Thomas: AT THE COPA! COPACABANA-A-A-A-! Anything?

Edna: No. Better knock it off, Thomas.

April 5, 2007: 2:37 p.m.

Edna: Thomas! We've got a group of young people entering the square. I'd say at least 20, Thomas. They seem to be moving with quite a purpose.

Thomas: Here it comes, Edna. Protesters most likely, possibly anarchists.

England's given them the shirt off its back and they stomp all over it. What are they doing now?

Edna: Let me zoom in. It appears they're holding hands, two by two and the leader is urging them forward.

Thomas: Probably chained themselves together. I'll give the crafty bastards the what for! *(audible microphone click)* YOU THERE!

Edna: Stand by, Thomas. They can't be more than ten years old, except for the leader; she looks to be in her thirties.

Thomas: HALT! DO NOT TAKE ANOTHER STEP UNTIL I GIVE THE ORDER. STATE YOUR BUSINESS HERE IN MIDDLESBROUGH!

Thomas: What is she saying?

Edna: Can't make it out. Let me open the window. *(sound of window opening)* WHO ARE YOU AND WHAT ARE YOU DOING IN THE PUBLIC SQUARE?

Outside voice: Alice Wilkins, headmistress of the Pinebrook Academy and we're taking a class trip to see how they make scones over at the pastry shop. *(sound of window being shut)*.

Thomas: *(audible microphone click)* DO YOU HAVE A PERMIT TO HOLD HANDS?

Edna: Doubt it's required, Thomas. She's won this round.

Thomas: GET MOVING! YOU THERE! NO SKIPPING!

April 5, 2007: 3:53 p.m.

Thomas: Over there! Stray dog milling about but …no sign of an owner, though.

Edna: *(audible microphone click)* ATTENTION, ATTENTION! THERE IS A

DOG OFF ITS LEASH. IF THIS IS YOUR DOG AND YOU ARE WITHIN THE SOUND OF MY VOICE, COLLECT HIM OR HER IMMEDIATELY! I REPEAT, COLLECT THIS STRAY ANIMAL IMMEDIATELY OR WE SHALL HAVE IT IMPOUNDED! THIS IS YOUR FINAL WARNING!

Thomas: Doesn't look like anyone's even in the area. Looks like he's having a bit of a lie down.

Edna: *(audible microphone click)* SHOO! SCATT! GRRRRRRRRRRR.

April 5, 2007: 4:59 p.m.

Edna: Check out this couple coming out of the pastry shop. That man's got to be more than 400 pounds.

Thomas: Why do people let themselves get so fat? Passive form of suicide, as far as I'm concerned.

Edna: I never thought of it that way, Thomas, but I think you're right. Suicide's illegal, isn't it?

Thomas: Of course.

Edna: *(audible microphone click)* YOU THERE, IN FRONT OF THE PASTRY SHOP! SPIT OUT THAT. Zoom in a bit, Thomas; I can't see what he's eating.

Thomas: It's a pastry of some kind. Has glazed sugar all over it.

Edna: Dear God. *(audible microphone click)* SPIT OUT THAT PASTRY, AND REMOVE YOURSELF TO HOSPITAL FOR IMMEDIATE PSYCHIATRIC EVALUATION. TOSS THE REST OF YOUR PASTRY IN THE BIN. YES, THERE! AND GET SOME HELP. YOU HAVE YOUR WHOLE LIFE AHEAD OF YOU! I REPEAT. YOU HAVE YOUR WHOLE LIFE AHEAD OF YOU!

Thomas: Look! You've even got him jogging a bit. Well done, Edna. You've saved a life today, you have.

Edna: You're too kind, Thomas. I'd say we've both done our part to keep the peace today, haven't we?

Thomas: We have at that, Edna. *(audible microphone click)* OI SONNY!. STOP BOUNCING THAT BALL AGAINST THE SHOP WALL OR YOU'LL BE BOUNCING IT INSIDE SPRING HILL LOCK UP! We have at that.

GETTING TO THE HEART OF VALENTINES DAY

Saturday is Valentine's Day but I'm betting you know that already. Probably completely prepared, right?

Me? I got some ideas working. Might head out to the mall. Pick up a box of candy. Everyone loves sweets and one size fits all unless you've got will power issues. Maybe one of those red velvet cards...

Who am I kidding? I'm never prepared for Valentine's Day because I don't get it. Every year Valentine's Day comes around and every year I feel like I'm being slapped with a romance subpoena demanding that I declare my love and my savings to everyone I've ever met.

I have to buy cards and gifts for my children to give to their classmates, their teachers, their friends, their grandparents. I'm supposed to purchase something for my wife, my daughters, co-workers and my mother. What's the significance of this sloppy, all-inclusive holiday anyway? If Valentine's Day is about romance, why in the name of Sigmund Freud and Oprah Winfrey must I send something to my mother? Isn't that why we have Mother's Day?

Judging by what people spend on this holiday, I may be the only one on the planet who remains in the dark as to what we're celebrating when we celebrate Valentine's Day.

According to the National Retail Federation's *2011 Valentine's Day Consumer Intentions and Actions Survey* (romantic title, no?), Americans spent $15.7 billion on cards, candy, flowers, jewelry and meals, averaging out to nearly $116.21 per individual.

That's nothing. Young adults between the ages of 18-24 are the biggest spenders, averaging $155 apiece. For the sake of those poor kids, let's hope the relationships last as long as it takes to pay off the credit cards used to purchase all those expressions of love. Love? What's love got to do with it? This is big business, baby.

"But John, you're just being cynical." Maybe you're right, whoever just said that. Perhaps I've spoken to soon. Maybe I should go back to the beginning to understand the origins of Valentine's Day before passing judgment. You can come to; just don't get too chummy. The last thing I need is another person I've got to buy something for.

The story of Valentine's Day is one in which fact and legend are intertwined – just like blind dates. Beginning in the 4th century B.C., the rites of passage of young men to the pagan god Lupercus were celebrated in a lottery where teenage boys selected the names of teenage girls out of a box to establish romantic relationships for a period of one year.

Some 800 years later in 496 A.D., Pope Gelasius wanted the church to distance itself from such pagan rituals and commanded that the names of young women be replaced with the names of saints, with the intention that young men would forget all about girls and choose to emulate the saints they selected. You don't need a market research firm to tell you how that went over.

Undaunted, the Church continued to seek a more suitable representative for romantic love than a pagan god, and reached back in history to 270 A.D. to summon Valentine, the bishop of Interamna, who had been clubbed and beheaded for his devotion to lovers and the sacrament of marriage.

Valentine had raised the ire of the Roman emperor Claudius II, known far and wide as a certifiable lunatic (but not to his face), who abolished marriage as a means to strengthen his armies. Claudius believed that married men made poor soldiers who preferred staying home and cleaning the gutters rather than poking strangers with sharp objects who often poked back with sharp objects of their own. Without wives at home, Claudius reasoned that men would welcome the diversion of invading another country on the weekends instead of say, bowling.

In defiance of the decree, Valentine continued to marry couples in secret until Claudius found out. Impressed with Valentine's conviction and integrity, Claudius attempted to convert Valentine to paganism as a means to avoid execution. Valentine, against the strong protests of his attorney, attempted to convert Claudius to Christianity. Although Claudius made a half-hearted gesture of flipping through a Christian pamphlet Valentine had given him, Claudius remained a pagan and Valentine held fast to his belief in God and the sanctity of marriage.

During his imprisonment, Valentine fell in love with the blind daughter of his jailer and reportedly through his unyielding faith, miraculously restored her sight. Before his execution, he signed a farewell message to his beloved, "From your Valentine."

So Pope Gelasius resurrected Valentine to serve as a romantic role model and after a time, pagan gods faded away and Valentine's Day became known as a church holy day.

Now I get it. If that's not a holiday intended to celebrate romance, call me Claudius. You can send Valentines and gifts to who ever you'd like but me, I'm going to write a little love letter to my wife and that's it. I love you too, Mom, but if you're craving chocolates, we're talking mid-May at the earliest.

THE BAD NEWS CALLER

Did you ever have a friend or a relative that seemed to derive great satisfaction in passing on bad news?

The phone rings. You answer. "Hello?"

"It's Martha. Didn't you go to high school with a George Tartuffo?"

"George Tartuffo. Tartuffo? Yes, I think I remember the name but I can't picture his face. Why, what about him?"

"Died Sunday. Some sort of freak boating accident. Apparently a Boston Whaler fell on top of him while he was standing underneath it at the Boat Show in the Javits Center."

"My God, that's horrible."

"Tragic... Thought you'd want to know. Gotta' run. Heading out to yoga."

Thought I'd want to know? Why didn't you call me when George won a Buick after hitting a hole in one at Baltusrol? Who wants to hear bad news all the time?

Apparently, if you read the papers or watch the news regularly, the answer is everyone.

I don't know if scientists have determined our psychic capacity for bearing bad news before beginning to suffer its ill effects, but I do know that I'm close to exceeding mine. Call me a crybaby but I could use a little good news. Something a little life affirming, a little ying to the yang of murder, deceit, hatred and greed —the four horsemen of the fourth estate. How about a couple of stories that reflect our capacity for kindness, generosity, tolerance, and forgiveness? Surely there are some of those humming along the newswires.

Who knows, maybe more stories involving kindness, generosity, tolerance and forgiveness could dupe us into thinking hope has a shot of unseating apathy and despair. Any takers?

Hello, Hollywood, CNN, the New York Times. Any good news to report? Anything? Dog raises kittens? Community joins forces to rebuild house destroyed by fire? Sorority girls videotaped in Florida during Spring Break teaching ESL classes? Any new programs on the horizon that don't revolve around murdering someone in cold blood, being murdered by someone in cold blood or catching someone who's murdered someone in cold blood?

Isn't it enough to have countless real life murders covered in rich, gory detail on the news each day – are our cravings for violence so great we need to create fictional murders as well? Week in and week out, the most consistently top rated programs are CSI, CSI Miami, Law and Order and Law and Order: Special Victims Unit.

Regarding local news organizations, I don't understand the point of being informed of every murder that occurs within their beat. What benefit does that news serve except to create a climate of fear? They say most murders are acts of passion committed by people who knew their victims, so the odds of them murdering me are slight to none unless I'm inclined to strike up a pen pal relationship with a convicted killer in prison – and believe me that's not going to happen -- I'm having a hard enough time trying to get this column in each week.

Have you noticed how most nightly news shows try to end on an up note after twenty-eight minutes covering news events that generally reflect the actions of people demonstrating the most abhorrent attributes of human nature? Right before the news team signs off with a little patter and a smile, you'll get a thirty second story about a nine year old national spelling bee winner who miraculously managed to spell "connoisseur" while her braces were stuck together. Recipe for perfect evening news broadcast: Mix nine parts angst and despair with one part hope and or levity.

When I contemplate the direction the media continues to take with its coverage of the news, my thoughts turn to the words of songwriter Nick Lowe:

As I walk through

This wicked world

Searchin' for light in the darkness of insanity.

I ask myself

Is all hope lost?

Is there only pain and hatred, and misery?

And each time I feel like this inside,

There's one thing I wanna know:

What's so funny 'bout peace love & understanding?

Don't ask me...

THE CATALOG: A MODERN FABLE

Once upon a time, the lovely wife of a man who secretly disliked the act of recycling sent a humble request to an enchanted place called Land's End.

The wife asked the caretaker of Land's End to send a catalog that provided a visual depiction of its wares thus making it easy to select garments without having to travel to department stores whose workers were feared throughout the Kingdom for their surly attitudes and unnatural ability to vanish into thin air at checkout time.

As was the custom between the man and wife, each night before they went to sleep they conversed, often laughing long into the night by carefully steering clear of subjects pertaining to financial matters, neglected tasks or the raising of their children. They were very happy.

Lo and behold the catalog arrived in the wife's mailbox. She became smitten the instant she saw the model on the cover dressed in a Georgette Flare Skirt, made from "an exceptionally lovely fabric" coveted far and wide for its ability to "waft on the slightest breeze". The wife was pleased to see that the woman was about her size, very pretty and yet not threatening.

That night when the husband entered the bedroom, he found his wife immersed in the new catalog. Settling into bed, he began a funny story about a man he saw at the train station that had accidentally closed a newspaper vending machine on his tie and unable to raise his head more than a couple of inches, politely asked passersby to borrow the 75 cents necessary to free himself. Expecting a big laugh from his wife, the husband was somewhat disappointed when she didn't react at all but leaned over with the catalog and inquired, "Do you think I could pull off this three quarter sleeve Coral Reef stretch shirt?" He fell asleep that night to the sound of flipping pages.

The next day the husband came home to find 175 catalogs stacked along the kitchen counter like the first row of a cinderblock foundation. All of them were from Land's End. There was Land's End Kids, Land's End Men, Land's End Home, Land's End School, Land's End Women, Land's End Women Plus Size, Land's End Women for Women Who Like to Dress Like Diane Keaton, and dozens more.

The husband confronted his lovely wife and asked her why she would order so many catalogs. The wife denied requesting additional catalogs and told her husband that she was just as shocked as he was about the unexpected arrival of unsolicited catalogs and could he please help her carry them to the bedroom.

That night there was little conversation at all. The husband drifted off again as his wife flipped through the dozens of catalogs that littered their bed, awaking with a jolt each time he heard the slap of another one hitting the floor.

The next morning, the husband rose before dawn and quietly gathered all the catalogs in the room. He tied them together with twine and hid them in the garage until the time came for them to be recycled. He hoped his wife would forget all about them. He prayed they wouldn't be recycled into new catalogs.

Three weeks passed and life had returned to normal. The husband and his lovely wife resumed their pleasant bedtime conversations and laughter once again filled the room – except when one of the children would barge in without knocking.

On the evening of the next day the husband returned home and was shocked to find 687 catalogs stacked along the counter. None of them were from Land's End. Enraged, he began to fling the catalogs around the room. "Pottery Barn. J. Peterman. Solutions. The Territory Ahead. Talbots. Travel Smith. Boston Proper. Victoria's Secret. Frontgate. I'd have to work around the clock like a coal miner to recycle all this!" he shouted.

His wife heard the commotion and rushed into the kitchen. Unable to calm her husband, she called for her children and together they tied him up with some twine and placed him in the garage to cool off while they went out for a bite to eat.

His patience restored, the husband noticed a Land's End Men catalog he had missed lying on the garage floor. Out of boredom, he began flipping the pages with his feet until his wife came back and untied him.

That evening, the husband's lovely wife leaned over to her husband and said, "While you went about it totally wrong, you were right about all those catalogs getting in the way of our marriage. I'll get rid of them first thing tomorrow."

The husband smiled. "I knew you'd understand. Just don't toss this one yet," he said, reaching for a catalog on the nightstand, "I'm thinking about this Pale Jonquil Drifter Crew. Do you think it would make me look washed out?"

And the good people at Land's End lived happily ever after.

IF WE'RE LATE FOR CHURCH AGAIN, I WILL KILL YOU

Do you know what a paradox is? Doesn't matter. I'm going to give you an example any way. A paradox is when a family comes within a hair's breadth of killing each other in order to attend mass on time and emerge afterward with a feeling of peace and spiritual reaffirmation. In addition to being a paradox, it's also a recurring theme --at least in my family -- where the hardest part of getting to God's house is getting out of ours.

As shocking as it may seem, the biggest obstacle standing between God and my wife and me are our children. They view mandatory church attendance the same way an accountant views the tax code – there has to be a loophole somewhere.

Growing weary of their jailhouse arguments every Sunday, I introduced a behavior modification program built upon ten simple rules that came to me during a vision in which God said, "Write this down and then get thee to Kinkos." We call it the Ten Commandments for Getting Through Church in One Piece. Here it is in its entirety.

I.   Thou shalt not feign death when awakened for church.

II.   Watching the 700 Club does not "count".

III. God does not take the summer off and neither shall thou.

IV.   Do not ask for whom the bell tolls for it tolls for thee if thou makest

THE BARBER'S CONUNDRUM AND OTHER STORIES

us late.

V. Thou shalt sit in one geographical area without constantly switching with thine brother or sister.

VI. Woe is the child who standeth on the kneeler when thy parent attempts to lift it up.

VII. Thou shalt suffer in silence when not chosen to place the envelope in the offertory basket.

VIII. Thou shalt not crush into powder the Cheerios spilt upon the floor by thine little brother or sister.

IX. Thou shalt not exclaim loudly, "I can't understand a word he's saying," during a priest's homily.

X. Thou will receive thy final reward in the form of Boston crème donuts if thou abideth by these commandments.

My wife and I read the commandments out loud to our children this past week and waited for a reaction that never came. They said they didn't want to comment until they had a chance to go over everything with their lawyer.

ROAD HOGS AND OTHER HIGHWAY CREATURES

A glance in my rear view mirror. Nothing within a 100 yards. A second later I glance again and there is a silver Lexus so close, I can see the driver's had one of his teeth capped. I look again and the car has disappeared. Where did he go? My left eye catches a silver blur and what looks like a sneer from the driver as he hurtles past me at 88 miles per hour. In an instant the blur turns back into a Lexus as the car jerks violently into my lane 18 inches from my front bumper and then comes to an abrupt stop. Yes, he is the victor today. He has beaten me to the tollbooth.

A recent Harris poll indicates that more than 62% of workers surveyed say they are unsatisfied with their jobs. A long-standing statistic on the state of marriage in this country states that one out of every two couples will be divorced.

As a recent petrified member of the automobile commuter community, I have one question. If almost everyone hates their job and or is stuck in a miserable marriage, why are they in such a desperate rush to get to work in the morning and to return home every day? Shouldn't the highway be the one place they'd find a little peace before facing whatever unpleasantness awaits them at the office or at home?

It's not working out that way. Maybe it's the personalities of the people who drive like maniacs that contribute to such dreary statistics. Who knows? I do know that there is only so much you can do to protect yourself even when driving defensively and if the popularity of the Humvee is a response to current highway conditions it won't be long before they're retrofitting drive-through banks to accommodate tanks.

I've identified four distinct driving behaviors on the highway.

The first is the "King of The Highway". Members of this group, in which there are generally two types of vehicles, believe they "own" the left lane. The first are high priced luxury cars and high end SUVs. Their message to those who dare drive in front of them is essentially rock, paper, scissors. "Get out of my way! Can't you see that my BMW 735 trumps your Infinity G35?" The second vehicle is the pickup truck. Their message is simple enough. "Get out of my way. I got nothing to lose."

"Video Game Road Warriors" is the next behavior type and the most frightening. These are drivers without any conception of reality. Weaned on video games, they weave in and out of traffic at tremendous speeds with no rationale. You may be in the left lane going along with bumper to bumper traffic and one of these maniacs will suddenly appear out of nowhere and attach themselves to your bumper. A moment later they spot an opening of 13 feet in another lane and burst across at hyper speed. In a second or two, you pass them, for you see there is nowhere to truly go in bumper-to-bumper traffic unless one has a vehicle in which you can pull back on the steering wheel and ascend into the sky. Another moment later the maniac is behind your car again, subconsciously pulling back on the steering wheel as their eyes dart about maniacally in search of another opportunity.

I'm a member of the third behavior group, "The Middle of the Road". All we want to do is travel nine miles over the speed limit in the center lane to retain our small fish status with the State Police, use our cruise control for more than fifteen seconds at a time and leave a nice healthy distance between those in front of us and those behind to avoid being crushed like a beer can when traffic hurtling along at an average of 75 mph drops down to zero.

I find the greatest risk of chain reaction car accidents occur when people slow down to read "critical" traffic alerts on computerized road signs. Note to the state highway authority: It's ridiculous to post two paragraphs of information to someone traveling at 65 mph. I'm waiting for the day they post a warning that says, "Caution. Reading this sign may result in unnecessary traffic delays and multiple car pileups."

The last driving behavior ironically enough is the sanest of the four and yet perceived by the other three groups to be the most mentally unbalanced on the road today. I refer to the "55 mph Set", the driver in the right lane who dares to simply obey the speed limit. This poor creature is the still life of the highway, ridiculed and dismissed by those who sail by, antagonized and bullied by those who are trapped behind them, tailgating menacingly in search of an opening to prevent the passing of cars they've taken great pains to pass only moments before.

After driving for more than 25 years, I've come to the realization that it's the 55 mph set that deserves the greatest respect on the highway. They are the rabbit and the hare story for the new millennium. Calm, reserved and steady and yet courageous and defiant in their resolve to ignore haste for haste's sake.

Keep a spot open for me boys, I'm about to catch up.

CAREGIVING APPLIANCES

I have a stereo receiver from Aiwa, the Japanese electronics manufacturer, and when I turn it off, the little LED window tells me "goodbye". The receiver is part of our home entertainment system --a term which could really apply to lots of things -- but now appears to be exclusively linked with consumer electronic products dedicated to enhancing our visual and auditory pleasures.

Eighty years ago, a home entertainment system could have applied to a pet monkey dressed up in a bellhop's outfit but today it's pretty much confined to music, movies and TV. It's too bad. I always got a good laugh seeing a monkey sporting one of those brimless red hats and a little blue jacket with gold buttons, but the odds of finding one of them next to the plasma screen televisions at Best Buy are slim to none. Believe me I checked, and after sitting through "Neighborhood Watch" three weeks ago, watching a fez wearing monkey fling all the condiments from my refrigerator around the kitchen sounds like entertainment Heaven.

But in lieu of a monkey, I have a home entertainment receiver that tells me goodbye when I shut it off. I find it intriguing that an appliance is programmed to speak to me completely out of the context of its intended purpose which is to amplify sound waves, tune-in radio stations and not blow up.

The receiver doesn't say "hello" when I turn it on. Nor does it occasionally ask, "Is everything OK?" during the middle of a movie, or

"Did you read the book?" Just goodbye – that's it. And even though the receiver and I have been together for more than three years, it has never once opted for a "Bye-Bye now." or "Have a good one."

At first I was upset – I mean what does it take to get an electronic device to let its hair down -- but then I realized that it could just be an aspect of the Japanese culture, which as you know is very formal. I can respect that. I'm not one who wants to see the whole world Americanized and saturated with the type of slang expressions that used to drive William Safire bonkers, I mean crazy. Goodbye is plenty good for me --especially when you take my VCR into consideration.

It's also an Aiwa -- an FX 8000 but it doesn't speak to me at all. I purchased it at the same time as the receiver and I find it odd that one Aiwa component is apparently willing to establish a deeper relationship with me while another machine seems content to keep things on a more professional basis.

They're physically connected to each other via cables, exchanging signals, working in close quarters. One admittedly formal but personable, the other closed lipped, content to be a loner. It's like that movie with the two convicts chained together, "The Defiant Ones."

Remember that film with Sydney Potier and Tony Curtis? A classic. They'll probably remake it with Ben Stiller and Vince Vaughn. Two words of advice. Save your money.

Anyway, with my Aiwa DVD, when I turn it off, nothing. No thank you or good bye. I even checked the manual to make sure everything was connected properly. It was. What can you do? To some appliances, it's nothing more than a job. To my Aiwa FX 8000, I'm just another faceless, nameless schnook without the common sense to go out and get some exercise.

And then sometimes I think: What if it's me? Maybe I'm being too hard on my DVD player, maybe it's just shy. Maybe I should try to get a little closer, use one of those DVD cleaning machines to give it a a tune up from time to time, let it know I care.

I looked into counseling for the DVD player and me, but whenever I asked a potential therapist how far away the electrical outlets were from where they'd be sitting, they all said the same thing: they weren't taking on any new patients.

Lately, my relationship with the entertainment system has worsened. The tension in the family room has become palpable, I'm no longer certain that my receiver is being sincere when it tells me goodbye and I'm convinced the DVD machine is scratching my daughter's iCarly episodes on purpose.

I'm thinking seriously about putting the whole entertainment system up for sale on Ebay and looking for an electronics company based in Vermont. They don't speak unless spoken to up there and when it comes to a home entertainment system, that's exactly what I'm looking for.

Or maybe I'll just see what Ebay's got in the way of monkeys.

Goodbye!

BEHOLD THE GOOSE

I was driving down a major avenue in my town the other day when I had to slam on the brakes to avoid running over a couple of Canadian geese. There were four geese and they were walking across the street like an avian version of the Beatles' Abbey Road cover.

My first reaction as I watched them waddle slowly past my car was to reflect on how cute they looked holding up traffic, oblivious to the world around them. I could see the lady in the car behind me – she was grinning from ear to ear. And the man who had stopped on the other side of the road was also smiling, making eye contact with me to let me know that we were witnessing something special. I grinned right back at him, equally captivated by this whimsical moment and then an instant later the pilot light must have reignited in my head because it suddenly occurred to me that Canadian geese fly.

Here were four mature, able bodied geese in the prime of life and when faced with a two thousand pound automobile bearing down on them at 35 miles per hour their God-given natural survival instincts trigger this reaction: Continue to walk slowly into the path of the speeding vehicle.

Nature's majestical beauty at the crossroads of industrialized society went right out the window, these geese were enjoying a laugh on us and I felt like a chump sitting there in my car while they took their own sweet time crossing the street.

I gave the horn a brief blast to see if that would remind them about their special gift of flight. No reaction except from one goose who actually flicked his wing under his chin at me as if I were a cop issuing a parking ticket and he was a foreign diplomat with immunity.

As the last member of the Brahmin goose class finally made its way to the other side of the road, I hit the gas and headed home unable to shake the notion that the modified behavior of these recalcitrant geese was directly related to what they had learned from us suburbanites.

Let's take a look at how this change in instinctual bird behavior must occur. We begin in Canada but not in the part where they speak French because I'm already over my head trying to pretend I know anything about biology.

A flock of Canadian geese are living in the wild. Baby geese follow the parents everywhere. (Refer to "Make Way for Ducklings" pages 1-8 for a more detailed understanding.) One morning a Canadian wolf enters the area in search of lunch. The geese elders responsible for security begin to honk. The parent geese react quickly to the announcement of imminent danger by concealing the goslings that can't fly. Those mature geese who've decided to delay children for a bit to enjoy the company of their mates simply flap their wings and sail into the sky, free and clear of any dangers outside of the rare possibility of being sucked into the engines of a 747. There it is. Natural survival instincts the way God intended.

One day an internal alarm clock goes off in the brains of every goose in Canada. It's time to migrate south for the winter. After stopping by the Post Office to have their mail forwarded, they take to the skies in the form of a giant letter "V" which contrary to what the advertising people would love for you to believe is not an endorsement for Virgin Atlantic Airways.

Some of the geese land in New Jersey. I'll let you draw your own conclusions there. These are wild geese mind you and one morning, a lady is walking her Malamute (a dog that resembles a Canadian wolf) through the park. The geese in charge of security honk, the Malamute charges forward and the entire flock takes to the air. But one goose happens to notice that the Malamute's charge was short lived, as the poor thing is now lying on the ground gasping for air at the end of a leather leash. Whether it's mental telepathy, genetic recoding or newsletters, somehow this goose tells the other geese that a wolf on a leash is a wolf that can be ignored.

No predators, no need to fly any further. And then the two-legged creatures begin to show up on a regular basis and feed the geese. Do you know how this is interpreted? "The two-legged creatures think we're gods," one goose declares.

A skeptical goose says, "You're out of your mind, they don't think we're gods."

"I'm telling you they do," the goose reiterates.

"Prove it, wise guy", says the skeptical goose.

"Watch this," says the goose with the God complex and he strolls across the avenue to the tune of screeching brakes and gentle sighs…

We're nothing but a bunch of goose enablers. It's a good thing all the dinosaurs are dead. We'd probably be down by the tar pits right now feeding them geese.

MAKING HOMEWORK HISTORY

Boy Breaks Homework Record

History was made the other day when ten-year old Owen Montgomery completed his homework in five hours and two minutes, shattering the record of five hours and six minutes established by ten-year old Alex Floss in 1937.

Here is the account of the spectacular feat as recorded by Owen's father, Eddie:

2:45 PM. Owen, who is in fifth grade and his sister Michelle, who is in third, burst through the front door and into the kitchen battling valiantly for possession of the last pudding cup.

3:00 PM. After two tiny servings of pudding, my wife announces it is time for homework, signifying the moment where the paths of brother and sister diverge even though they remain less than a couple of feet apart at the kitchen table. Michelle follows the path leading to the completion of her homework while Owen pretends his pencil is a robot.

Note: Michelle loves school and her homework is always complete, always correct, and with penmanship so neat, you'd swear her imaginary friend was a typesetter. Owen is very bright but hates homework, and when confronted with it, displays the symptoms of someone who has been in a room filled with ether. While Michelle is finished within the hour, that is often the minimum amount of time it takes for my wife to fully comprehend what my son's homework assignments are for the day, and which books needed to complete those assignments are still sitting in his desk at school.

4:00 PM. After comprehending what Owen's homework assignments are, he and my wife return to school to retrieve his math workbook and social studies book.

4:30 PM. My wife explains to Owen that his math homework requires him to show the mean, median, mode and range for the list of numbers in his workbook. Our son explains to his mother that he remembers the terms but not exactly. My wife admits the same and asks to see the math book. Our son informs her that the math book is at school. My wife asks him to explain why the math book is in school when she asked him not more than half an hour ago to identify what books he needed for his homework. Owen gets up to sharpen his robot. My wife instructs him to start on his social studies homework while she searches the web for the math information.

4:50 PM. My wife returns and asks to see the social studies homework Owen has been working on for the last 20 minutes. He says, "I thought you only told me to get the book out."

5:05 PM. Owen is allowed to come out of his room. Math homework recommences.

5:15 PM. Owen excuses himself to use the bathroom.

5:30 PM. My wife runs upstairs to find out if our son has collapsed in the bathroom. Luckily he is still alive and watching TV. His vital signs are strong.

5:45 PM. Owen is allowed to come out of his room. Math homework recommences.

6:18 PM. Math homework checks out and dinner begins. Everyone seems to be having a good time except my wife, who refuses to look up from a travel magazine.

6:27 PM. Dinner ends abruptly to make way for social studies. Owen must memorize all the U.S. states and capitals and where they exist on the map for an upcoming test. My wife instructs him to begin writing down all fifty states in alphabetical order so he can memorize them first. Owen insists he doesn't need to write them down, he knows them all already. My wife asks him to identify them.

6:28 PM. Owen begins to write down the names of all fifty states…

7:00 PM. Social studies ends and English homework commences. Owen must write the spelling words for the week five times each and then use each word in a sentence.

7:30 PM. My wife examines his spelling first. She informs me that our son has an excellent chance of becoming a doctor because his penmanship is almost completely illegible. She tells Owen to rewrite the words. Owen insists he doesn't have to do that because the teacher never looks at the words. My wife starts to speak but then opts for her more ominous stare, which compels our son to begin his rewrite.

8:00 PM. Exhausted, my wife asks me to review Owen's sentences while she searches for a bottle of schnapps she remembers receiving last Christmas.

8:10 PM. Owen presents his completed sentences to me.

8:12 PM. Two are closer to haiku poems than sentences but I let it slide after one look at our son's beaming face as he realizes homework is finished and it's not even 8:30 yet. Our son has shattered the world homework record for ten-year old boys!

Not one to rest on his laurels, Owen intends to break his own record again this year and believes his chances are excellent if he can convince his mother to stop meddling.

HOUSE OF WAX

Last Sunday, I took my son and five of his buddies to celebrate his birthday at Madame Tussaud's Wax Museum located right in the heart of the theatre district in New York's Times Square.

We drove over in my Taurus station wagon. That's right, six normal sized 12-year old boys and me. For you super sized SUV owners who might envision my car as a four-wheeled version of a '50s phone booth stuffing stunt, it may surprise you to know that the little Taurus has room for eight – alright seven if you prefer securely storing a drink somewhere other than on top of the roof.

I have never been to a wax museum before and knew nothing about Madam Tussaud's outside of the fact that like all tourist attractions, its bylaws entitled me to leave the museum exhausted, penniless and with the vague but insistent notion that the employees snickered at me whenever my back was turned.

In an attempt to forestall the snickering until we at least entered the exhibit, my wife scoured the Internet for discounts and found one where I could purchase two adult tickets at $25 and receive one child ticket free. According to her calculations, the total cost should have been $119, but the cashier charged me $144. I don't know why, I only know the line behind me was growing longer and more cantankerous as the exasperated cashier puzzled over the promotion for more than twenty minutes until finally coming up with a magic number of $144. The transaction took so long, I can only assume the additional $25 charge was for lodging.

We were finally inside after strolling past a twelve-foot wax replica of The Hulk, which to me was an odd choice to start off with considering there is no real life equivalent of The Hulk. What can you say? "Wow! He looks exactly like… that cartoon character in the comic book. Alright, let's see what else they have."

Next we entered the Opening Night Party exhibit, where anyone who is anyone and attached to the floor with bolts was in attendance. We saw Woody Allen, Bette Midler, Nicolas Cage, Hugh Grant, Oprah, even a wax version of Jennifer Lopez, who rumor has it was briefly engaged to a wax version of Harrison Ford.

The likeness, and attention to detail is incredible and even though the figures are made of wax, I didn't see even a hint of a wick protruding from anyone's head. Whoopi Goldberg was there as well and looked so lifelike, I'm convinced that if she had sent her wax figure to that Democratic fundraiser for John Kerry instead of herself, no one would have known the difference and she'd still have that nice endorsement position with the Slim Fast people.

After the party we waited in an excruciatingly slow line for the Chamber of Horrors, an exhibit which cost an additional $3. As we stood in place for more than fifteen minutes listening to endless audio loops of actor Hugh Jackman's fruitless pitch for his poorly received movie "Van Helsing", I overheard my son Jack mutter to his friends that they should have called the attraction the Chamber of Waiting.

I wish I could tell you what we experienced in the Chamber of Horrors. It was dark, there were real people dress liked ghouls who mumbled incoherently like Popeye, occasionally I noticed sacks of something hanging from the ceilings, and then less than a minute and a half after we entered, we were propelled into a brightly lit room like moles suddenly exposed to the sun and when our pupils finished dilating, the first thing we saw was a wax replica of NBC Today's Al Roker, prompting my son's friend Ben to say, "Now it's really getting scary."

There were dozens of other famous wax figures from the world of sports, politics and entertainment but after a while it started to feel less like a museum and more like a department store to me. Also as a public service announcement to avoid the sort of heart breaking disappointment I witnessed in a family of apple growers who had driven all the way from Canada -- there is not and I repeat not -- a single exhibit featuring wax fruit.

For me the most impressive site of all was the figure of the black clad, diminutive wax mogul Madame Tussaud herself. If made to scale, she was a very tiny woman, and could have made one heck of a living as a jockey. But she turned a job making wax replicas from the heads of France's countless victims of the guillotine during the 18th Century into one of the most popular tourist attractions in the world. As we turned for the door, I gave the old Madame a little pat on the back to acknowledge her entrepreneurial spirit, and at that very instant I heard this spine tingling, high pitched cackle.

Does anyone know what a snicker sounds like in French?

THE NEXT BIG THING

There was an article in the *New York Times* this week about an executive from a Silicon Valley venture capital firm who staged a contest called "Pitch Tim Draper on Your Billion Dollar Idea". Mr. Draper's intention is to uncover and conceivably fund business opportunities that are innovative, unique and marketable.

For example, one of the finalists presented an idea to mass-produce flying cars with retractable wings. Could you imagine? Flying automobiles? The only thing that could possibly be more exciting than flying to work at 2,000 feet alongside thousands of other commuters in two-ton automobiles with retractable wings would be flying alongside thousands of commuters in two-ton automobiles with retractable wings who are also attempting to dial their cell phones at the same time. Gosh, with an innovation like that, could underground pedestrian walkways be far behind?

I must say that news of the competition inspired me and I found myself coming up with dozens of scientifically feasible ideas to submit including one called the "Contest Ending Retractor" --a reverse time continuum device specifically designed for people who need to go back in time to prevent missing deadlines for contest submissions as I apparently did when it turned out Mr. Draper's contest ended three weeks ago.

While I sadly lack the funding for aluminum foil or the necessary garage space to build the Retractor at this time, a little Internet research revealed that the "Pitch Tim Draper on Your Billion Dollar Idea" contest is an annual event. I now find myself in the enviable position of having a full year in which to submit my concepts – all 128 of them, which are already fleshed out in great detail on 3x5 index cards and attached securely to the refrigerator with magnets.

Here's a sneak peak of my top four, billion dollar business innovations.

The Flat Vacuum Attachment. This revolutionary home maintenance device, which is six inches wide but only one sixteenth of an inch thick, would attach to a normal vacuum hose and be used to extract valuable items from hard to reach places – say a 3x5 index card from underneath a refrigerator, for example.

The Living Hotline. A voice recognition device designed to reach the living. Here's how it works. You simply dial a number to a company, say the phone company for example, and then leave the room to make better use of your time while the Hotline navigates through the hundreds of automated, pre-recorded customer service prompts, the phone company, for example, believes enhances and simplifies your customer service experience. When the Hotline makes contact with the living – otherwise known as an actual human being in the employ of the company you are trying to reach, it notifies you with an audible beep. Tangible benefits: Saves time, lowers blood pressure, reduced risk of using bad language around minors.

The Miracle Laundry Hamper. This spring loaded device has built in sensors that detect dirt levels in clothing to prevent washing clothes that are already clean. Here's how it works. A child puts on a perfectly clean shirt to attend church and upon returning, attempts to stuff it into the hamper to avoid hanging the garment up properly. Lifting the hamper lid instantly activates the sensors and within one tenth of one second, they analyze the shirt for stains, dirt or signs of foreign matter. If none are detected, the hamper projects the clean garment back at the child at a speed of 110 mph, thus initiating a conditioning process designed to eliminate the bad habit completely within 3-4 days. Tangible benefits: Save time and money on laundry, develops strong hand-eye coordination in children.

The Polly Want a Polygraph. Potentially the greatest revolutionary breakthrough in political accountability since the invention of the hidden camera and the abolition of dueling. Here's how it works. A polygraph machine is housed within a replica of a parrot that is attached to the shoulder of every elected official above the position of alderman. When the politician speaks, the machine measures the physiological response and in the event deceptive behavior is detected, the parrot shrieks "Bra-a-a-ach! He's lying through his teeth. He's lying through his teeth. Bra-a-a-ch! Tangible benefits: Promotes honesty in government, high entertainment value, raises awareness about parrots.

Great ideas, right? Wish you thought of one yourself? Don't worry about it. Stop by the house around this time next year; I'll take you up for a little spin in my flying Ford Fiesta.

EVERYTHING I LEARNED I LEARNED FROM MAGAZINES

Hello friends. Do you ever wonder why there is never enough time or money to do the things you know deep down you'd like to do? To decorate your homes, travel, invest wisely, sculpt your body, add romance or raise your children without resorting to methods more commonly associated with members of the animal kingdom.

I'll tell you why. You're not reading enough magazines! This weekend I corrected every problem I've ever had with my life not to mention 74 I didn't even know I had – simply by reading magazines at the bookstore.

You were on my mind the entire time. In fact I made a list of the most significant, life transforming articles you'll ever have the great fortune of reading, assuming you can find them between the ads.

Transforming your life does require a bit of work so before we get started, I suggest you read *Lifetime Magazine's* "5 Secrets Of Nonstop Energy" first. Better do it now. I'll wait.

Wow, you look positively radiant. Let's get physical.

If you need an exercise plan that doesn't require more than a half-hour, consider *Fitness Magazine's* "Single, Best 20 Minute Workout". While I'm sure it is the best, otherwise they wouldn't say that, I went with *Outside Magazine's* "The Only 10 Workouts You'll Ever Need". Exercise ten times and then be in shape forever? I'm in.

Many articles allow you to transform your physical appearance quickly. If you have only minutes to spare, *Allure Magazine* offers "Kicked Back Beauty – 2-Minute Hair And Makeup". If you have but one minute, there's "The Minute A Day Method To Perfect Shape", from *Jane Magazine* and if you have no minutes, *Women & Home Magazine* shows you how to "Look 5 Years Younger Now", *Men's Fitness* provides "30 Ways To Look Great Right Now", and *Self Magazine* authoritatively offers "The # 1 Way To Look Prettier Instantly."

If time isn't an issue but having a number of options is, I suggest "789 Great Health, Sex, Fitness & Nutrition Tips", from *Men's Health*, "546 Style Trends For You", from *Perfect Hair Magazine*, "200 + New Looks For You", from *Seventeen*, "42 Muscle Building Meals", from *Men's Fitness*, "25 Fat Burning Shortcuts", from *Exercise And Health*, "9 Ways To Dine Out And Lose Weight", from *Allure*, and "5 Sandwiches That Build Muscle", from *Muscle And Fitness*.

To show how these articles have already altered my life, before I read "5 Sandwiches That Build Muscle", I used to make sandwiches without any strategy whatsoever and built muscle by carrying my kitchen table to the park, eating my sandwich there and then hauling the table home again. All that time wasted and never knowing how little I knew about love.

To enhance your romantic skills, I suggest you first read "Find Your Signature Scent" in *Body & Soul Magazine*. Every little edge helps, particularly if you're a man --because magazines make it clear that there is nothing as mysterious and unknown as women.

Before reading "187 Things You Don't Know About The Other Sex" in *Esquire*, "11 Sex Dreams You Need To Know About" in *Cosmopolitan UK Edition*, "8 Ways To Reignite Postpartum Passion" in *Pregnancy Magazine*, "7 Myths That Could End Your Marriage" in *Psychology Today* and "The 31 Sex & Love Thrills No Women Should Miss Plus 6 Bedroom "Musts" You Can Skip" in *Glamour* -- you may wonder as I once did -- if the Hubble Telescope is pointed in the right direction. Have no fear. They've explained everything there is to know and now that all women's secrets have been revealed, I suggest all of us (that includes men and women!) focus on beautifying and organizing our homes.

If the inside of your house is a mess, I suggest you start with the outside. If there are no bodies of water on the property, I suggest "10 Reasons Why You Need A Pond" from *Ponds USA*. I was hooked as soon as I read reason number 3, "It's a great place to conceal old tires, rusted lawn furniture and the occasional murder victim." For those of you who have a backyard but are no longer elated when standing in it, *Do Magazine* humbly offers "3 Ways To Enjoy Your Backyard".

Turning our attention inside, *Oprah Magazine* shows you how to get outside again with "Stop Morning Chaos. 12 Ways To Get Out The Door Quicker". If you must stay indoors, and want to challenge yourself, why not consider "47 Projects To Do This Weekend" from *Better Homes And Gardens' Quick And Easy Decorations*, "100 Ways To Unclutter Your Home", from *Organizing Good Things*, or for those of you looking for appliances as role models for your children, *Dwell Magazine* offers insight on "How To Find The Perfect Oven".

Worried that your household is so dysfunctional it's affecting your pets? Make the diagnosis today by reading *Cat Fancy's* groundbreaking treatise "When Cats Mourn – 7 Signs Of Grief".

Now if all this self-help information appears overwhelming – relax – there are articles to restore serenity to your life such as "You Got Stress? 1,000 Time Savers, Mind Savers – Just For You." from *Redbook* and *Good Housekeeping's* "Moody? Anxious? The Medical Test You Need Now!" to determine whether your goofy personality quirks betray deeper, more serious medical concerns.

I hope you pick up these magazines. A new life awaits you, really. Me? I'm 100 % more energetic, insightful, successful and organized. As a matter of fact, during the entire time I was writing this article, I was also reading *Field and Stream's* "50 Ways To Fool Spring Trout". Turns out they're a sucker for those lose weight while you sleep schemes.

PROOF OF ALIEN LIFE ON EARTH

Irony of ironies. We're spending billions looking for signs of life on other planets and aliens from outer space are already here. Yes, space aliens! They've been here since the mid 80's and they've taken over almost the entire customer service industry. How do I know? For one thing, I've conducted exhaustive research and for another I hear voices in my head, which can be an excellent source of information once you sort out who's who.

Let me emphasize that space aliens do not have it out for us, their physical makeup and cognitive abilities are simply not suited to our planet or to the tasks required to provide adequate customer service.

Now if you promise to reserve judgment to the end, I promise to make believers out of all of you by citing several deficiencies in the physical makeup of space aliens which correspond directly to specific examples of horrible customer service we've all experienced. And no snickering under your breath, I'm providing valuable information for free. It's not as if I'm charging you $2 billion to reveal the mysteries of Martian dirt. Dirt. Here we are spending tens of millions of dollars each year on door mats and dust busters to get rid of dirt and NASA's spending hundreds of millions to get it. That's the government for you. Anyway, back to my theory on how space aliens have taken over the customer service industry.

Aliens from outer space have remarkably poor eyesight and hearing. Ever walk into a store and not have a single employee acknowledge your presence even though you heard the little bell ring above the door as you entered? When an employee is on the phone in front of you but fails to make eye contact to let you know that they know you are there, do you ever pinch yourself to confirm that you are an actual physical entity and not a wraith from the spirit world in search of a curtain rod? Don't worry; you're completely human. The employees? Aliens from other planets. While they see each and hear each other just fine, witness the jolly, jabbering conversations they have while you stand unnoticed before them, space aliens cannot differentiate between animate or inanimate earthly objects.

Aliens from other planets can't distinguish human voices on the telephone. Ever had a real conversation when calling the phone company, a department store, a consumer product company or government office? If your answer is yes, consider yourself lucky. You reached a human being. If you ever hear the automated words, "Your call is important to us," that's a company run by aliens from outer space. Hang up and don't try again!

Earthly foods create confusion in space aliens. Ever been to a restaurant where the waiter takes your order, taking great pains to go around the table one by one? Later someone else comes out with your food and proceeds to ask each person at the table who had what until all the food is cold and the once witty and bubbling dinner conversation is replaced with sullen requests to reheat dishes and whispered accusations as to whose idea it was to come to this restaurant anyway? Humans can both take dinner orders and hand out food, distributing the right dish to the right person. Space aliens experience disorientation when handling food. Scientists have not pinpointed the exact cause but theorize it may have something to do with the uncanny resemblance between the head of their galaxy and calamari.

Aliens from outer space can't comprehend mathematics. Ever hand a twenty dollar bill to a person operating a cash register to pay for an item that costs $10.53 and then admittedly at the 11th hour, hand that person another dollar bill so you could receive a ten dollar bill and .47 cents in change? If that "person" begins to mop its brow, mutter profanities and glare at you as if you were one who recommended that they absolutely must see "Paul Bart, Mall Cop", rest assured that "person" hails from another planet.

62

Aliens from outer space have no conception of time as we know it. Ever said this to a friend who has invited you over for dinner? "Thank you for your thoughtful invitation! I will be there sometime between the hours of 5:30 p.m. and 1:30 am. Please confirm that you will be home and the meal will be hot during that time." Of course you've never said that! If you're human. Now, have you ever ordered phone or cable service and the representative informs you that someone will be at your house between the hours of 9:00 am and 2:30 in the afternoon? Got to be people from other planets, right? No conception of time whatsoever, let alone human courtesy. Need further proof? Do they ask you to wait at home for six hours when they shut off your service for failing to pay the bill? No way. Why? Humans handle that side of the operation.

Through a chemical reaction in the body, space aliens convert oxygen into ether creating a somnolent physical state (commonly referred to as the "Where in God's Name Did They Go?" syndrome) in which all mental and physical response rates are slowed dramatically. The cashier asks a colleague for a price check on a sweater. The colleague disappears only to return 15 minutes later with the price for a pair of culottes. You make the universal "Bring me the check" pantomime to your waitress. She smiles, nods affirmatively and then disappears for so long you have to file an Amber Alert. Studies indicate that for every minute it takes a human to complete a task, it takes a space alien 17 minutes, with the exception of the South where it takes them 34 minutes.

That's it. I rest my case that it is aliens from outer space who have made a shambles of our once proud and heralded customer service industry. I'm also hearing rumblings that they've infiltrated Congress. You may now snicker at will...

A MOUSE TALE

Last Thursday, my wife and I were coming home from my daughter's triumphant performance in the third grade production of "School for Cupids", when we spotted a mouse making its way through the snow in our front yard.

I told my wife that it seemed strange to see this tiny black mouse in a field of white, particularly since animals are supposed to be so well versed in the art of camouflage to avoid predators who prefer protein over carbohydrates.

My wife was not intrigued and refuses to meet any of God's creatures unless they are caged, taxidermied, served next to vegetables, or reconstituted into clothing and accessories. While nature may abhor a vacuum, my wife abhors nature. She also abhors vacuuming but I know for a fact she'd use one if it were to vacuum up a mouse. Which brings me to my point and the source of my guilt.

Our family had mouse trouble, I had put out some poison and it was certainly a possibility that the little mouse in our yard might be familiar with our basement.

I had my camera with me so I decided to take his picture. Why? Who knows? Maybe to tease a cat. I do know the reason I had my camera was to record my daughter's performance. It is now required by law to document every single event in your children's lives or face the consequences, the worst of which is having other parents look disapprovingly down their viewfinders at you and making a "clucking" sound with their tongues.

Let me state for the record and for my daughter who will find out soon enough when she sees the prints, that darling, I tried desperately to capture the essence of Miss Lovejoy's kind and mentoring manner in your enchanting performance, but the blocking and stage direction was such that I never saw anything but the back of your head until the curtain call. I know it wasn't your fault, sweetie, I blame the entire educational system.

As I moved closer with the camera, the cute little mouse remained oblivious to me and I began to worry that he had eaten the poison. The pellets cause mice to become terribly thirsty and the desperate need for water drives them outside where their thirsts are ultimately quenched. In Mouse Heaven. These pellets offer no reprieve for trespassing and a first offense is always the last. Now that I was up close, this mouse seemed worthy of a second chance.

Yes I know --I put out the poison, yes I wanted the mice out of my house and yes, I still felt quite remorseful -- and for that I blame my father, the closet Buddhist from Jersey City.

When my brothers and I were little, if a moth was spotted flapping frantically against a lampshade or crawling across the TV, we'd reach for a newspaper, rock solid in our authority to dispatch any insect to the spirit world.

And then one day my father walked in the room while I attempted to evict a moth with a copy of TV Guide and said, "Don't kill that moth. For all we know he could be out looking for work with a wife and 600 kids at home waiting for him to come back." Dumbstruck, I watched as he gently cradled the moth in his hands, opened the window and sent him back to his family.

That was it for me. From that point on every insect, every rodent, every pigeon, every moth became an individual. I began to picture them in their nests, Norman Rockwell scenes of cricket babies learning to hop, groundhogs sipping ice cream sodas in underground drug stores, ants constructing their little colonies with the purity of heart and steadfast devotion of the Amish.

I became a bipolar, neurotic link in the food chain . No worries eating lamb chops or chicken breasts but hold that shovel so I can move this worm out of harms way. The circle of life turned into a cul-de-sac and it is there that I still reside.

So here was this mouse that, thanks to the good people at D-Con, was supposed to just disappear without a trace. Maybe he passes away, maybe he wins the lottery and moves to Scottsdale – who would know for sure and for me that was the beauty of it. The only way I'd known he'd existed at all was when I removed an empty pellet container. But not this one. He had to emerge from the crowd of unwanted pests and show a little personality.

I used a shovel to scoop him up gently along with a pile of snow and carried him down to the river, trying to convince myself that maybe he was alright after all, just a little disoriented. And that's where I left him, ambling along the riverbank toward whatever fate has in store.

It's a week later, I still have mouse poison in my basement and with all the things in the world there are to worry about, I'm still worrying if the mouse made it. My kids think I'm nuts but that probably has more to do with my replacing their picture over the mantle with the mouse's.

THE TIMES THEY ARE A CHANGIN'

My wife and I met another couple in New York the other night to have a rare adult's night out – an occasion generally categorized as one in which a group of parents leave their children at home and then spend the entire evening talking about them.

For our adult night out, we went to see Los Lobos perform at Irving Plaza, meeting first at a restaurant to have a drink, a little dinner and to talk about how we weren't going to talk about our kids like everyone else. Actually, I think that was all we had time to cover before the show started.

Los Lobos hails from East Los Angeles, and has been playing a mix of rock and roll and traditional Mexican music for more than thirty years. Take it from me, they're terrific. That is if you want to take it from me. It's fine either way, you're not going to hurt my feelings. My kids never take my word for anything so I'm used to being ignored or contradicted. Just wait till they have to ask me to put up our home for bail money. Fat chance...

Anyway, I was very excited about seeing the band live because their music elicits fond memories of my days living in Del Mar, CA in the mid eighties --which is where I first heard them. I was a flat broke college graduate without prospects, a girlfriend or medical benefits, collecting a meager salary as an extraordinarily inept construction laborer forbidden after the first day on the job to operate any tool requiring electrical power and driving a rusty, ten year old Pinto station wagon that leaked oil like a hatchback version of the Exxon Valdez. Gosh those were great times. I couldn't wait to relive them.

Irving Plaza is a tiny club that stands roughly 800 people, since there are no seats to be had on the main floor. It is literally wall to wall people and the quickest way to get a laugh is to mention the term "personal space" to the woman who's purse is cutting off the circulation to your spleen. If you ever hear about a performance being held in an intimate setting, don't assume it has a thing to do with the size of the room.

The opening act was a soulful troubadour who reminded us so many times between songs that he was a working class guy from Las Vegas, I began to wonder if there was going to be a pop quiz at the end of his set. "Before I do this last song, would you mind passing these number two pencils to the people standing in the back by the bar?" Thankfully he finished up, twenty minutes later Los Lobos came out and I was shocked.

There is a comedian named Emu Phillips who told a joke that went something like this: "The other day I saw this kid from my third grade class, Timmy Wilson. I ran up to him and said, 'Hi Timmy, how've you been?' and then I realized, wait a minute – if that's Timmy Wilson, he would have grown up too."

Los Lobos had aged! The lead singer's hair was completely gray as was the base player's. The music was the same, maybe better but the band moved very little on stage as if to conserve energy. At the end of the night some of the band member's sons came out to play along side their fathers. They looked to be in their twenties.

How old are these guys, I wondered. If they aged, doesn't that mean I aged? What a stupid question, of course I aged. I looked around the room. Almost everybody who had come to the show was in their late thirties and forties. Surely they looked older than I did. Didn't they?

I started yearning to see the young troubadour again. Sure he was a kid but he didn't have any connection to when I was a kid. Los Lobos looked my age when I saw them twenty years ago. I wonder if *they* think they still look the same.

I leaned over to my wife and yelled in her ear, "Do those guys look older than me?"

"What?" she yelled back.

"DO THOSE GUYS LOOK OLDER THAN ME?"

Just then this beautiful young woman who had been standing next to me all night and smiling brightly each time our eyes met, gently tapped my shoulder and leaned in close, placing her lips next to my ear. "Excuse me sir, but would you mind lowering your voice, I can't hear the music."

I think that's it for live performances for a while. Unless it's Willie Nelson. I know I look younger than that guy.

POLITICIANS

Solving the Character Issue

In this emotional political season where divining the true character of our political candidates is more difficult than telling the cleaners where to deliver Jean-Bertrand Aristide's pants, I find my thoughts turning first to spring, simply because I've about had it with winter and then to Richard Nixon, the first political sacrifice made to the pagan gods of television.

Nixon lost the 1960 presidential race to John F. Kennedy, in large part due to his "performance" at the first televised political debate. While most viewers polled after the debate agreed that Nixon had a solid handle on the issues and clearly outlined his political objectives, the same viewers felt his physical unease before the cameras, five o'clock shadow and pale complexion left them uneasy when compared to JFK's confident, media savvy demeanor, and beautiful tan.

Well, you know how it turned out: the pale, nervous, awkward guy was narrowly defeated by the robust, charming, media savvy guy.

Lesson learned and 40 years later everybody that runs for office is the robust, charming and media savvy guy – except the women – they're the robust, charming, media savvy gals. Can you still say that, "gals"? I better apologize in advance. Anything publicly stated beyond "Hello" these days often results in a class action suit. Before you get any ideas, everything I own is in my dog's name and everything he owns is in the Caymans.

Moving on, how are we supposed to sort out this new breed of politician who knows just as much about lighting their good side as they do about supply side economics? How can we really know what a political candidate truly thinks when their off the cuff remarks are written six weeks earlier by a team consisting of six Harvard graduates, Dr. Steven Hawking, Camille Paglia, two fellows from the Rand Institute and a couple of kids from The Simpsons?

Until this year, I couldn't have cared less either way. I've been a registered member of the Baby With the Bath Water Party for over a decade. We believe it is in the country's best interest to reject all individuals seeking higher office on the basis that no one in their right mind would want to run in the first place.

But that's not a political ideology to pass on to children and more importantly people stopped inviting me to election night parties and I really miss that five-layer Mexican bean dip which never tastes the same when I make it at home.

So I came up with an idea that might help us skeptics get back into the political swing of things. A mandatory, three-month reality television series on C-Span that follows each candidate everywhere they go. It's perfect. No one, not even the most seasoned political animal can stay in character 24/7. All us voters would have to do is tune in and wait for the façade to crumble.

Want to know whether George Bush is telling the truth when he says his wife is his most trusted advisor? Let's see how he handles the clicker when they're both sitting on the couch in front of the tv.

Want to substantiate John Edward's assertion that he knows how difficult it is to juggle job and parenting responsibilities? Let's watch how he reacts to the realization that the water dripping on his eggs from the ceiling is the direct result of his son flushing a Beany Baby down the toilet.

Would you rather hear Dennis Kucinich's rationale for decreasing the budget deficit or listen to the explanation he gives his wife after learning that the last check he wrote for a plasma screen TV was $1800 more than what they had in their checking account?

Want to know whether Al Sharpton has the organizational skills to implement a voter registration program? Let's see how he puts his clothes away at the end of the day. Does he hang everything back up neatly? Does he toss everything on the chair oblivious or unconcerned about the risks associated with bad feng shui ? Or is he possibly a hamper man like my son, who creates the illusion of neatness and responsibility by simply tossing everything in the laundry - clean or dirty -just to avoid hanging anything up at all?

For the record, my wife nor I will never vote for someone who knowingly stuffs perfectly clean clothes in a dirty clothes hamper.

I believe a C-Span series that follows presidential hopefuls around the clock for 90 days is the cure to our collective political malaise. I say forget the speeches, the policies, the platforms and the platitudes, there's no need for us to know whether they really feel our pain or not. Let us see how they handle their own pain in the form of the trials and tribulations we all learn to live with each and every day.

Show me a man who can stay to the end of a birthday party with twenty-seven screaming eight-year old boys and I'll show you the potential leader of the free world.

Can I count on your support?

HERE A PRODUCT, THERE A PRODUCT

As I sit here at my iMac, organizing my iLife, which provides all the tools I need to work outside the office – quite frankly I don't know how I got by without it --I want to share with you an exciting advancement in the world of product placement. Product placement, the practice of featuring commercial products prominently in movies and television programs, including Law and Order, the show whose exciting stories are ripped straight out of today's headlines, has now expanded to include "chick lit".

For those few of you out of the know, chick lit is a new term for a style of romantic fiction that appeals to young women. For example, "Bridget Jones Diary", written by Helen Fielding, recently made into a charming and wildly successful motion picture from Miramax starring Renee Zellweger, is an example of chick lit.

It has nothing to do with Chiclets, the gum. Yet. "Say, how about a Chiclet to go with that chick lit you're reading?" Wow, that just popped into my head! I wonder what they would pay for a product tie-in concept like that? I'm going to run down to Washington DC on the Amtrak Metroliner, now operating with 75% less accidents, and get that copyrighted before somebody steals my idea.

I'm back, but I must tell you that there is nothing that calms your nerves after a harried trip to our nation's capital than a Starbucks Grande Tazo Chai Tea, mmmmm. I actually feel one with the world and for only $3.85.

Chick lit and product placement. Here we go. The marketing visionaries at Ford Motor Company came up with the brilliant idea to pay British novelist Carole Matthews to mention their cars in her novels and short stories. Her latest book, "The Sweetest Taboo" features her Ford Fiesta that she calls Flossie. The Ford website, which I managed to click through easily and seamlessly using Microsoft's Explorer internet browser, reports that "The Ford Fiesta comes alive in the pages of "The Sweetest Taboo" and will also star in a selection of short stories that Carole is writing ...[which] will be snapped up by women's magazines and national newspapers."

According to the BBC's World Business Report, Ms. Matthews states that whenever her heroine is driving a car, it will now be a Ford Fiesta. "That's the only thing they've asked me to do, they've placed no other constraints on my writing at all," she says.

Gosh, all that cash up front and no constraints. I would love the opportunity to write a major novel after striking a deal with a major corporation, but I'm not cut out for novels. I hear you have to stay up late, drink and chain smoke and I know I don't have the discipline to keep that up for long. I'm more of an idea guy, which is another way of saying there might be an angle for me to get rich in this new industry without knowing anything or doing any real work. I'll tell you how, if you promise not to email, phone or direct connect to anyone using your BlackBerry 7510™ until I return from the copyright office via the Amtrak Metroliner, now serving premium Bigelow teas.

I've launched a new company called Literary Product Placement Matchmakers®. I'm going to contact the authors or copyright owners of the world's most beloved novels and ask them to ever so slightly rewrite their books to mention some of the world's most beloved products.

Take "The Adventures of Tom Sawyer" for example. There's a scene in the beginning of the novel where Tom has to paint a fence and he's just about conned his buddy, Ben into helping him complete the job. Here's what's in the book. "Say, Tom, let me whitewash a little," Ben begs.

Here's what we add. "Whitewash? Ben, this here's Benjamin Moore Autumn White, with a 15-year guarantee not to fade, crack or peel for gosh sakes – this ain't no whitewash! It's a good thing Aunt Polly didn't hear you say that, she'd box both our ears!"

Ka Ching!

How about "The Godfather" after poor Sonny Corleone was shot to death at the tollbooth at Jones Beach? The phone rings, Corleone consigliere Tom Hagan answers and hears on the other end: "Sonny's dead, they got him at the Jones Beach toll."

We add: Hanging up, Tom cries to the heavens, "Poor Sonny, if only he listened to the family doctor and corrected his violent mood swings with Prozac® Weekly™, he'd probably be home with Mama right this very moment making pies. "

Here's your check, Mr. Hartnett and thank you.

How about that old children's classic, "Green Eggs and Ham"? Remember this: "Would you? Could you? In a car? Eat them. Eat them. Here they are. I would not, could not, in a car."

We add: "Unless it is a Ford Freestar. With a 3.9L SPI V6 and overhead cam. I'd gladly eat green eggs and ham!"

The possibilities are endless, just like the beautiful, tranquil sunsets my wife and I would like to experience at Club Med Sandals® resort, created exclusively for couples in love. Anybody from Club Med reading this article? Call me. Please?

TEN COMMANDMENTS FOR RESTAURANT OWNERS

An Open Letter To All Restaurant Owners:

Do you know the number one reason most restaurants fail within their first year of business?

They deserve it, that's why.

I know that sounds harsh but you have to understand that when we come into your establishments, it's because we're paying for a dining experience we can't get at home. Our expectations aren't high –all we desire is a decent meal, a little service and the peace of mind that comes from knowing we don't have to drag the Shopvac up from the basement to clean under our children's chairs. That doesn't seem like too much to ask, does it?

Apparently it is. Lately, I find the only way to get through a terrible dining experience is to imagine myself eating in one of the seaside cafes depicted in the expensive murals that cover the walls. Many's the time I've "disappeared" into a charming Italian villa by the sea while waiting for my missing waiter to reappear with the bill.

But I'm not here to just complain about the state of the restaurant industry or to encourage greater use of murals that showcase charming seaside communities that stimulate daydreaming as a means of overcoming unpleasant customer service experiences, I want to help – particularly those entrepreneurs considering whether or not they have what it takes to open a new restaurant.

So here are ten helpful tips from a seasoned diner to make sure your restaurant lasts longer than a Whoopi Goldberg talk show.

1.   Always greet people when they enter your restaurant. Customers love this because it reinforces their belief that they are actually alive and can still be seen by others.

2.   Customers appreciate it when a waitperson tells them their first name when they approach the table. This makes it much easier to seek additional support when their waiter or waitress disappears without a trace. "Have you seen Lance? We're still down three entrees and about to draw straws to determine who's going to plaster his picture on telephone poles."

3.   Most people consider a dining experience to be a positive one when their entrees all come out at the same time. The only exception to this rule is when you serve customers who view unsynchronized meal delivery as a wagering opportunity.

4.   While many waiters and waitresses are aspiring actors, encourage them to write down the specials if they can't remember them. Seasoned diners can spot an improvised specials speech a mile away. "Our Ahi tuna is served piping hot in a reduced balsamic …um, seafood glaze with olives, anchovies and uh, a tiny medallion of tapioca pudding."

5.   Make sure the tables are set and never underestimate the feeling of comfort people derive from knowing that their eating utensils are all present and accounted for when they are first seated. Have you ever tried to have a conversation with someone missing a knife and a fork at a restaurant? Monosyllabic answers to detailed questions, eyes darting nervously about the room searching for someone, anyone to bring them utensils before the food arrives, muttered open ended questions with no easy answers like "Where is this guy?" One missing fork can spoil an entire evening and you haven't even brought out the meal yet.

6.   If you run a family restaurant and members of your family work there it always helps if they pretend to actually like people. As an example, parents with children rarely return to a family themed restaurant if the owner uses a throat slashing gesture from behind the register to communicate that the use of crayons is frowned upon.

7.   At this stage in our human existence, it is no longer necessary to include photographs of food as a means of describing them in a menu. People know what most dishes are supposed to look like and they never look like the dishes in the pictures anyway.

8.   While food presentation is important, if a customer can't decide whether to eat an entrée or have it framed – you probably shouldn't be in the restaurant business.

9.   A bill should never be delivered looking like a ransom note. If it's not uncommon to see a group of customers hovering over a bill like a heart transplant team, confiscate the pens and exchange them for pencils or even a computer – they're much less expensive now and often come bundled with encyclopedia software.

10.   When someone requests water from a waitperson, actually bring them a glass. They love that.

Ten surefire tips for restaurant success.   No charge, just a 15% gratuity which I took the liberty of adding when I assumed a party of six or more would be reading this. Hope I'm right.

SEND ME ALL YOUR MONEY, PLEASE

Would You Be A Dear and Pick Up $30 Million For Me?

Lately, I have been besieged by email scams from residents of foreign lands requesting my assistance and money to help them claim millions of dollars they have spirited away in a desperate attempt to escape a political coup or subsequent arrest as experienced by one or more of their unfortunate but wildly prosperous family members.

You've probably received similar pleas from distressed foreigners and have chosen to delete them. You shouldn't. Responding to these letters is a wonderful opportunity to hone up on your creative writing skills and should not be passed up. C'mon I'll show you.

First, here's a sample of one of the many letters currently clogging my email:

Dear Friend,

My name is Loi C. Estrada, the wife of Mr. Joseph Estrada, the former President of the Philippines. My husband was recently impeached from office by a backed uprising of mass demonstrators and the Senate. My husband is presently in jail and facing trial on charges of corruption, embezzlement, and the mysterious charge of plunder which might lead to the death sentence.

The government is forcing my husband out of Manila to avoid

demonstrations by his supporters. During his regime as president of Philippines, I realized some reasonable amount of money from various deals that I successfully executed. I have plans to invest this money for my children's future on real estate and industrial production.

My husband is not aware of this because I wish to do it secretly for now. Before my husband was impeached, I secretly siphoned the sum of $30,000,000 million USD out of Philippines and deposited the money with a security firm that transports valuable goods and consignments through diplomatic means.

I am contacting you because I want you to go to the security company and claim the money on my behalf since I have declared that the consignment belongs to my foreign business partner. You shall also be required to assist me in investment in your country. I hope to trust you as a God fearing person who will not sit on this money when you claim it, rather assist me properly, I expect you to declare what percentage of the total money you will take for your assistance.

When I receive your positive response I will let you know where the security company is and the payment pin code to claim the money.

Thank you and God bless you and family.

Mrs. Loi C Estrada

Here's the creative writing part and you don't have to worry about punctuation or anything, just let your imagination run wild!

My dear friend, Loi,

What a tragic story! To be pushed out by demonstrators is one thing, but the Senate? That's like Snooki telling you that you lack class. The whole episode just makes me sick! I want to give you everything I own right this very moment. Plunder. Of all the charges they could accuse your husband of, they had to choose plunder. He will now go down in history associated with pirates, the scourge of the sea and fairy tales everywhere. Captain Bligh, Captain Hook, Blackbeard, and now Joseph Estrada.

While I go into my bedroom to locate all the jewelry I plan to pawn on the behalf of you and your imprisoned spouse, I also encourage you to call an attorney in California named Robert Shapiro. If he can get O.J. Simpson acquitted of murder, surely he can get your husband acquitted of an offense that hasn't been mentioned since Charles Laughton won the Academy Award for Mutiny on the Bounty!

What ever happened to Imelda Marco's shoes? If you're friends perhaps they could be sold to raise bail. I bet the pumps with live goldfish in them would do great on Ebay. Oh, wait, you secretly siphoned some money away, didn't you? Siphoned. Now there's a word for our generation. If only your husband could have been accused of siphoning -- it just sounds more juvenile delinquent*ish* -- he'd be out in no time with a charge like that. They might make him write a hundred word essay and call it even.

Oh, but what's the use of trying to change what has already happened? In America, we say "Don't cry over spilt milk." What do they say in the Philippines? Wait, don't tell me. Tell me when you and I are sitting together in lounge chairs at the Nick Bolliteri tennis clinic in Boca Raton. Do you play tennis? Why Loi, you simply must! Tell you what. Send me three million of the $30 million you siphoned and I'll get you a racket and a case of balls. That's right a whole case, which normally costs six million. You can pay me the rest when we see each other face to face. I trust you.

As for the security company, tell me the address and I'll go first thing in the morning. Is it near where I live? Not to worry, I have a bus schedule! I won't let you down, Loi.

All my love,

J Edgar Hoover

Isn't that fun? Sadly they never write back but I guess that's a good thing. I'd pay Loi $30 million just to keep sending me dopey letters like that...

THE SCHOOL PROJECT: AN AMERICAN TRAGEDY

My wife and I do too much for our children and the guilt has become so overwhelming, I feel compelled to confess publicly in the hope that someone can guide us out of the dark, twisted labyrinth we disappeared in more than four years ago. The shame of committing countless clandestine acts, relying upon deceit, trickery, and cajolery for the sake of our children has become too much to bear and can no longer be justified by the need to get a decent night's sleep.

I refer of course, to the school project.

If ever there was a need for parents to unite against a common enemy it is the school project. I've nothing against reports but if a homework assignment requires plaster of Paris, glue, cardboard, cement, newspapers cut into strips, paint, clay, wood, beads or the use of arc welding equipment – let's return to an agrarian society where wheat was once ground into flour for food and not to serve as an adhesive ingredient in Paper Mache.

For those of you unfamiliar with take home school projects, or for those of you fortunate enough to have suppressed such memories, there are seven stages to every school project. Let me enlighten you:

Stage 1. The Introduction and the Delivery of False Hopes.

In this stage, a child announces at dinner that they have been requested to make a diorama, say one on the book, "The Jewel Princesses and the

82

Missing Crown". A parent, generally the mother, will announce gaily that she has been saving shoe boxes for such an occasion, in much the same way expectant mothers knit booties. There will be a brief discussion on how the diorama will be constructed, including the type of materials needed to ensure that it is as beholding to the eye as it is informative. A sense of confidence that all is in hand will fill the room. A parent will casually ask between bites when the project is due, the child will respond that it is due in one month and the parents will process that information to mean that they never have to be concerned about this again.

Stage 2. High Noon.

The night before the day before the project is due, the child will approach one or both parents and shriek, "What about my diorama?" One or both parents will respond, "Why did you wait until now?" There will be finger pointing, recriminations and the gnashing of teeth during this stage.

Stage 3. It Takes a Village to Decorate a Shoe Box

On the day before the project is due, work will be parceled out to all family and extended family members within a radius of fifteen miles. It will take no less than three trips to the local crafts store, the Home Depot of the elementary school set, to assemble all the accessories necessary to complete the diorama. A grandparent will be dispatched to locate a roll of contact paper once spotted in their basement six years prior.

Stage 4. We Are All Being Graded

The child will begin to assemble the diorama but it will not pass the standards set by the parent or parents who worry that the little 8" x 12" box could potentially be seen by someone they know over the age of eight. The Internet is dispatched and graphic items are printed in an enormous volume to provide the greatest number of decorating options. A sibling of the student will be reduced to tears when a beloved toy doll is surgically altered to fit inside the box. Negative emotions run high throughout the duration of this stage, despite claims that the maimed toy will be replaced, that future projects of such scope and magnitude will commence at the instant in which they are revealed to the parents, and that the bed is pretty much in scale with the armoire made from wooden matches.

Stage 5. Emerging From the Trial By Fire

Generally sometime after 11:00 pm, anger is replaced with a sense of accomplishment when the school project is completed. All the stress and turmoil evident on the faces of the parent or parents will vanish once it is apparent that the nightmare is over. A moment later, the stress returns when the child mutters that this is not how she would have done the project if she did it all herself.

Stage 6. The Return of the Prodigal Project

Days later the child returns with the project and the grade. Everyone celebrates the "A" they received. The project is placed in a position of prominence for a period generally lasting no longer than 72 hours before it is tossed into the trash with the coffee grinds while the child is at school. It is never missed nor spoken of again.

Stage 7. A Clean Slate

A child comes home with a new school project. Repeat steps 1-6.

I'm willing to march in front of the school board if you're with me on this school project issue. We can get everything we need to make signs at the Crafty Kitchen.

THE DOG DAYS OF SUMMER ACADEMY

Here's a very special offer from the Dog Days of Summer Academy for all you parents out there who didn't sign your kids up for any summer programs because you thought it would be important for them to experience the lazy, carefree days you remember so fondly as a child and are now petrified that something regrettable will happen if you hear the phrase "I'm bored" just one more time.

Leave it to the next generation to give the formerly endearing term "endless summer" a sinister new meaning. Not to worry. We'll make things right -- and for only $895 per student!

While there are thousands of summer programs that focus on athletics, academics and the arts, the Academy staff understands that it's you, the parent, who are paying the bills around here and should therefore reap the lion's share of the benefits derived from the skills we instill upon your children. That's why our program focuses on teaching your kids skills to make your life easier – not theirs. Sounds selfish? It is!

Sample courses include:

DDA-012 Short Order Cooking

(Ages 4-12)

Learn to wake up on the weekends quietly without disturbing your parents, enjoy the satisfaction of making your own breakfast, master the art of cooking crepes, eggs benedict, corn beef hash and for those of you too short to reach the stovetop, cereal.

(Prerequisite: DDA-213 Dishwashing)

DDA-362 The Telephone and You

(Ages 4-16)

Did you know that the telephone is one of mankind's most valuable tools? Harness its true power by learning how to write messages down and deliver them in less than 48 hours. Understand the importance of hanging up telephone extensions so that others may contact you or members of your immediate family.

DDA-815 Speaking to Adults (for beginners)

(Ages 4-16)

In this introductory class we will discuss the art of conversation between children and adults beginning and ending with the simple greeting that leads to more in depth conversations covered in **DDA-816 Speaking to Adults (intermediate)**. At the end of six weeks, when an adult relative or friend of your parents spots you on the street and says "hello", you'll be amazed to hear yourself say "hello" back in a clear, articulate voice!

DDA-101 Conflict Resolution for Siblings

(Ages 18 months to 18)

Did you know that screaming, bickering and knock down, drag out fights between siblings are the number one reason parents leave for vacations in the dead of night often without telling their children where they're going or when they'll return? This course provides a variety of techniques for restoring order in the house. You'll learn how to argue in silence using *The Mime Way*™, soundproof your tree house, file a restraining order, and for extreme cases, learn how parents can doctor birth certificates to enhance your eligibility for the Merchant Marines.

DDA-901 How to Prolong the Life Expectancy of Baseball Hats

(Ages 6-18)

In this simple, three minute class, we will explore the reasons why baseball hats which are consistently worn indoors in spite of parental requests to remove them disappear at a much greater rate than those baseball hats that are worn only when outside the home.

(Prerequisite: DDA-599 Introduction to the Knee and Its Role in the Classification of Short Pants)

DDA-472 Eating Meals at Home

(Ages 4-16)

This course is built upon an exciting role-playing game in which you play the parent and the instructors play your children. Points are awarded to the children's team whenever a "child" succeeds in ordering "off the menu", has to be called to the table more than twice, fails to wash hands before sitting down, refuses to eat healthier items, is able to persuade you to dish out dessert in spite of not finishing dinner, uses fingers in lieu of utensils and chews with their mouth open. "Parents" are awarded points if they are able to remain in the dining room without sneaking out to go on vacation.

Dog Days Academy classes begin next week. Your satisfaction is 100% guaranteed or we'll refund the entire amount or keep your children until they're 18. Operators are standing by.

AN UNWANTED GLIMPSE OF THE AFTERLIFE

Have you ever wondered where people go when they die? Heaven? Purgatory? How about a sound stage in Queens?

Apparently that's the liveliest place to meet dead people if you've ever seen John Edward's syndicated TV show *Crossing Over*. Mr. Edward is a psychic from Long Island who receives messages from the dead and then seeks out their friends and relatives in the audience to help him flesh out what the messages mean and to whom they are intended. If you haven't seen the show, get ready for a wakeup call, especially if you think you already know something about Heaven, the spirit world or just being deceased in general. I was very disappointed in dead people after watching my first episode. It's clear that Mr. Edward and I do not share the same vision of the afterlife, and with all due respect to everyone who has crossed over, if his version of the afterlife is it, I'm not going.

When I think of death, I envision that white light as described by those who have died and then come back to life. We ascend toward the light and then into Heaven where all earthly things fade from memory, reportedly none more quickly and God affirming than the image of Lindsay Lohan being placed into the back of yet another squad car.

Not so on *Crossing Over*. If you're looking for enlightenment and Heavenly insights from the great beyond, you'd have better luck getting it from recently deceased Lehman Brothers than *Crossing Over*. The dead, who appear to struggle against a din of spiritual chatter to capture the attention of Mr. Edward, conjure up an image of an afterlife that resembles not the pastoral peacefulness of a Heaven many of us envision, but New York's Port Authority Bus Terminal during rush hour. I was expecting clear, specific and enlightened communication from the afterlife, something along the lines of....

Mr. Edward: I'm getting a message from a Donald Westlake.

Woman in the Audience: Oh my gosh, that's me! I mean that's my grandfather!

Mr. Edward: He wants you to know, Elaine -- it is Elaine isn't it?

Elaine: Yes!

Mr. Edward: He wants you to know that there is nothing to worry about and to let go of all your problems because they are meaningless. He wants to assure you that your husband Dave will get the job with Citibank. He also wants you to know that Heaven is an incredible paradise and to let go of fear -- for you and your loved ones will all be together again for eternity -- which in most cases is perceived as a good thing. (laughing) I added that last part, Elaine. OK, let's take a quick break and then we'll be right back with more of Crossing Over!

Here's what you get on *Crossing Over*:

Mr. Edward: I'm getting something for a Tom, Tony, a common T sort of name. Tammy, Timmy, Tootie...

Man in the Audience: My name is Pete.

Mr. Edward: Ah, that explains the strong "T" sound. There is someone in your family who has passed from a tumor or blockage of some kind...

Pete: My Uncle Ray had a heart attack last year. Had a blocked artery, I believe it was.

Mr. Edward: He wants you to know about a light bulb or a lamp on a boat, perhaps a sailboat or a schooner, maybe a raft, canoe, hydrofoil? Anything nautical and electrical...

Pete: He had a table lamp he made from one of those old ship in a bottle kits. I broke it when I was visiting his house years ago. I must have been six or seven years old. I can't believe it's him!

Mr. Edward: He wants you to write your aunt a check for $33 dollars to replace the lamp you broke. He wants you to know that he's OK where he is, and to tell his son to wipe off the smudge on his picture above the fireplace.

Pete: Anything else?

Mr. Edward: No, but he seemed really upset about that smudge. Don't forget to tell your cousin. OK, I'm getting something about a Francine, Minerva, maybe Motorola … anybody own a Japanese TV? All right, I understand. Someone from the other side really wants to let a loved one know that a cable wire is loose and that's why the reception is so bad.

And that's TV's version of the afterlife. A bunch of dead people preoccupied with earthly matters so trivial, even the living don't know what the hell they're talking about. So much for my version of Heaven. When I picture Heaven now it's the Kramden's apartment from *The Honeymooners*, packed wall-to-dreary wall with dead people throwing elbows and screaming out the windows at the top of their lungs, "John! John Edward! Tell my son-in-law to put up the storm windows!" I said it once, and I'll say it again, if that's the afterlife, I'm not going.

THE PASSION OF HOLLYWOOD

LOS ANGELES, March 7 (EP Newswire) –Mel Gibson's "Passion of the Christ" continues it reign as the top movie at the box office taking in $51.4 million in its second weekend. The film has surpassed the $200 million mark in just 12 days.

Confidential Memo

To: Harry Mayburn, President, Pollyanna Pictures

From: Leo Wallace, V.P. Production, Pollyanna Pictures

Re: The Peaceful Buddha

Hi Harry,

Brilliant idea! Here's what I've been able to find out about Buddha so far. Overall, likeable guy with an excellent demographic of more than 613 million ticket buyers, I mean followers. Am I bad or what?

Before I get to the plot, there are some casting issues that could lead to a little marketing challenge. My wife has a statue of Buddha in the backyard and there's no getting around the fact that the mature Buddha has a bit of a weight problem.

I've got a couple of interns doing some research to see how he looked growing up, but if it turns out we have to stay with a chunky Buddha for the sake of authenticity, we're prepared to go with Val Kilmer for the later years. That'll skew well with the male demographic and then we just have to introduce a young, hunky spiritual apprentice for the ladies. I'm thinking Johnny Depp, Tobey Maguire or possibly Justin Bieber, although I heard a rumor he's actually 42 years old.

The good news is you're going to love the story of Buddha -- think "Prince and the Pauper" meets "Lord of the Rings" minus the $150 million they had to spend creating hobbit feet.

Buddha starts out as a prince named Siddartha around 500 BC. Young Sid is a bit of a dreamer and his father, the King – I'm seeing Russell Crowe, maybe Ben Kingsley, although I heard he's become a handful to work with after being knighted– is worried that his son is going to abandon the good life and his royal status to focus on religion 24/7.

Picture young Sid in a beautiful palace oblivious to the three dozen voluptuous beauties that pamper him and feed him dates like he's a sea lion at Marine World. He stares forlornly out the window watching the poor peasants suffering and dodging elephants in the courtyard below him. Sid feels their pain and vows to leave the trappings and avarice of high society to experience the real world on his own.

The king is so worried about losing Sid he marries him off to a charming beautiful princess, (perhaps Taylor Swift if we limit the lines, Scarlet Johannsen if we don't, let's discuss) and they spend 12 years together until Sid can no longer stomach the obsession with vanity and materialism.

Sid makes ready to leave, but his father stations guards at every door of the palace to prevent his escape.

Harry, according to our researchers, the day Sid is to leave, a supernatural event occurs. Thirty-three gods descend from the sky to put all the guards to sleep and hold the hooves of Sid's horse so he can leap over the palace wall undetected.

While quite an astounding feat, cinematically that scene is a bit of a yawner. For the sake of our crossover, action oriented, non Buddhist audience, I strongly suggest we substitute the "sleeping beauty" scene with a death defying "Matrix", "Crouching Tiger, Hidden Dragon" sequence in which Sid hacks and fights his way through a couple of hundred nasty, sword wielding guards before he makes it out of the palace.

The audience will go bananas at the end of that scene, guaranteed, so why lose that opportunity by sticking to a couple of high flying deities sprinkling Sominex on everybody? Leave that sort of thing to the highbrows over at Sony Classics.

So now Sid is thirty years old, living in austerity with the poor people and actually... that's all I have for now. We do know that somewhere along the line Sid changes his name to Buddha, and becomes a spiritual leader -- albeit with some diet related willpower issues, although who knows, it could be gout. Let's trust the writers and the researchers to do their jobs so we can focus on the important things like marketing.

Now since Buddha is known as a bit of a tree hugger, the marketing team is pushing hard for an Arbor Day opening. We're thinking about doing something with the Burpee seed people —maybe Buddha lotus seeds, we're still hashing it out. On the fast food side of the fence, we pitched a Buddha kid's meal toy made entirely of soy products but the execs were concerned that the toy would actually be more nutritious than their hamburgers. I told them we'd just stick with plastic.

I see nothing but green lights and greenbacks, Harry. God bless Mel! Wait, you're not going to believe this. One of the interns just came in and told me that Sid became a Buddha after being reincarnated many, many times. Harry, we've got a franchise on our hands!

SURVIVING YOUR FIRST TRADESHOW

I have a little greeting card company and paid to have a booth at the National Stationary Show this week at the Jacob Javits Center in New York. For me the purpose of the show is to generate sales, network and search for potential business opportunities.

To accomplish most of these goals, you just have to stand in front of your booth from 9 am to 6 pm and smile engagingly at every person who walks by. This isn't a skill they cover in business school; in fact I learned how to do it from watching a hairless Chihuahua work the room during pet adoption day at the pound. He lives in my town now and whenever I see him walking regally alongside the lady who selected him from that sea of adorable competitors he gives me a little wink. His name was Ray when he was in the pound but now it's Eduardo. If he's ever reincarnated and comes back as an insurance salesman, watch out.

You have to have thick skin to work a trade show. Often people walk by without so much as a glance and if you're not careful you can start to feel like a bruised pear in the produce section. Experiencing rejection at tradeshows is as guaranteed as rain during a family picnic but always tempered by conversations about the big deal – think Willie Loman meets Cinderella which translates into hope^2 for you math buffs -- and you'll have a pretty good idea.

Usually the big deal pitch comes from a tag team of impeccably dressed people from foreign countries who descend upon your booth like paratroopers, examine all your samples in great detail, and speak to each other in urgent hushed tones before turning their attention to you.

I've been in the publishing business for many years and the really big deals always had something to do with foreign distribution and translation.

"I represent 47 countries including their Epcot Center counterparts and we'd like to translate your product into every known language including one that is only communicated by using hand puppets and tapping on a hollowed gourd with a monkey's fibula. Unfortunately, we do not have a pen at this time but will be back tomorrow at 9:30 am to finalize everything before our flight at 9:35 am."

They never come back. For years I used to rush around looking for them in vain until wisdom finally intervened and I realized they were the gabardine clad equivalent of fool's gold. One day scientists in search of an elephant graveyard are going to burst through a clearing in the jungle and discover thousands of South American businessmen in blue suits wandering aimlessly with briefcases and screaming into cell phones with dead batteries. "You don't understand. I must get out of this place now. The Americans are waiting for my order!"

So in between the big tradeshow deal there are lots of time for just waiting. Lots of time for reflection and thought. This week I started to obsess about how thoughts actually appear in my head and who or what was responsible for creating them. The obsession began as I was standing in the middle of the aisle thinking about the opportunities that could be derived from forming a cooperative with other small greeting card companies when an instant later I began to wonder whether God gets offended when women second guess His creative genius by shaving off their eyebrows and drawing them in themselves with pencils.

Where does an unsolicited thought like that come from? To go from a very logical internal conversation well within the context of what I was doing to suddenly be interrupted with something so far out of left field, psychiatrists wouldn't know what to make of it.

The only explanation I can think of is that I had not had a chance to eat anything substantial and might have been suffering from some sort of food related dementia. The woman who was scheduled to work the tradeshow with me became ill and I had to work the whole show by myself. Since I could not leave the booth, I was forced to eat all six pounds of the Hershey Kisses we had originally purchased to pass out to attendees to avoid starvation. I must have been hallucinating because I vaguely remember slapping the hand of a woman buyer from Target, who attempted to remove one of the candies from the dish I was clutching protectively to my chest like Humphrey Bogart in "The Treasure of the Sierra Madre".

The effects wore off instantly however, when I received the biggest order of the day. Someone purchased twelve dozen of every design in my card line. I had the first big deal of my career. And to top it off, the guy who made the purchase lived in my hometown so I didn't have to worry about him disappearing into the jungle.

He introduced himself as Eduardo but told me his friends call him Ray.

ONLINE CHAT WITH SEARS OR HOW LONG DOES IT TAKE TO ORDER A REFRIGERATOR GASKET?

The Internet should have it's own ring in Dante's Circle of Hell. Here's my nominee for this year's *Woefully Less Than Adequate Online Customer Service Hall of Fame Award*. The following transcript of a chat session that I had with Chad from Sears this morning is verbatim with the exception of deleting some of my personal information and substituting "You", as my response was recorded in the session, to "Me". The basis for our online meeting? My desire to order a part for my old, Sears Kenmore refrigerator so that I didn't have to spend $500 to replace it. The refrigerator is in my basement, I use it mostly to store beer and 75 pounds of duck sauce packets I've saved since first ordering Chinese takeout n in 1992. You can laugh all you want, but they make great stocking stuffer gifts. Especially for people you'd rather not see again.

The conversation took the better part of 30 minutes before the transaction was completed. It starts out professionally and expediently enough and I think if Mother Theresa were alive today and sitting behind me reading over my shoulder while I chatted with Chad (ooh, I get goosebumps just thinking of her sitting over my shoulder on one of those stools with the seat that can spin up or down to increase its height) she would say I was very patient for as long as I could be until the conversation digressed to such a point that she herself, Mother Theresa, would have have pushed me aside to take a shot at Chad with a garden rake.

And so, without any further ado, I present to you "My Online Chat with Chad". Not to be confused with *"My Dinner with Andre"* — which was a movie that featured pretty good service if I recall correctly.

Please wait for a Sears Parts Direct agent to respond. This chat may be monitored or recorded for quality assurance purposes. Your average wait is 2 seconds. Thank you for holding.

You are now chatting with 'Chad'

Chad: Thank you for choosing Sears Parts Direct. My name is Chad. How may I assist you?

Me: Looking for a door seal for a Kenmore refrigerator — 1069618412 Kenmore 18 cubic feet, 18atr92 is the other code

Chad: Hello there.

Chad: I'll be more than happy to check and help you locate and order the door seal for your refrigerator.

Chad: Thank you for the model number. May I have your name, please?

Me: John

Chad: John, just to clarify, do you need the freezer or refrigerator door seal?

Me: Refrigerator

Chad: Great news! I have located the model specific door seal, for you and what's more you would get FREE 90 day warranty too.

Chad: To save your time and ensure you receive your part on time, I would be happy to place an order for you ensuring delivery to your home or business.

Me: Yes.

Chad: John, the guaranteed best price for your part with normal delivery, not including any applicable taxes, is $56.65

Chad: Would you like to place this order on your Sears card or Sears gold Master Card?

Me: No, another card.

Chad: No problem, we do accept all major credit/debit cards.

Chad: To quickly begin with the order, may I have your full name, phone number with the area code and your billing address, please? Also, are you a home owner?

Me: John Hartnett *(provided phone #, address)*

Me: Yes, I'm a homeowner.

Chad: That is great to know you are a home owner.

Chad: John, the shipping address same as the billing address, correct?

Me: Yes.

Chad: John, the guaranteed best price for your part with tax and normal delivery is $60.62

Chad: The normal estimated date of arrival on this order is Sep 22.

Chad: Please stay online till I provide you the order confirmation number.

Chad: John, while we are placing an order for your refrigerator, the manufacturer recommends cleaning the coils on your refrigerator once a month.

Chad: Performing this maintenance will help improve your energy efficiency.

Chad: We have a tool made especially for this task.

Chad: It comes with a long handle that will reach those hard to clean areas that your vacuum can not.

Chad: Would you like to improve your carbon foot print and order a coil brush today?

Chad: The coil brush is only $7.30

Me: No thank you. Also, can you expedite delivery of the seal?

Chad: Please keep this brush in mind the next time you place an order with Sears Parts Direct.

Chad: Yes, the expedite shipping date is Sep 19

Chad: Is that okay with you?

Me: How much is the difference in cost since we're only talking 3 days?

Me: The guaranteed best price for your part with tax and expedite delivery is $60.62

Chad: I'm sorry for the typo, John.

Chad: The guaranteed best price for your part with tax and expedite delivery is $73.44

Me: The 22nd is fine.

Chad: Sure, thank you.

Chad: John, do you have a refrigerator with water filtration system?

Me: Yes, but not this one.

Chad: I have a wonderful offer with which you can save $10.99 of your shipping fee on this order.

Chad: You can order as many parts as you would like with your order today and pay nothing for shipping!

Chad: Would you like to know how you can avail this wonderful offer?

Me: Chad, what I would really love to do is complete this transaction. Can you help me with that?

Chad: Yes, it will take only few minutes to let you know about the offer.

Chad: Is that fine with you?

Me: Sure, if immediately after, you'll let me spend a few minutes telling you all about the time I got lost at the mall.

Chad: I'm sorry to hear you have faced such a situation.

Chad: John, how often do you change your refrigerator water filter?

Me: Never, but I can't because of my religious beliefs.

Chad: The reason why I ask is because, the manufacturer recommends you to replace the filter once in every 3 to 6 months.

Chad: John, you can receive free shipping on your entire order today by just enrolling for our Water Filter Re-order program for your refrigerator,

THE BARBER'S CONUNDRUM AND OTHER STORIES

which not only saves you shipping charges but also ensures that your family gets germ free purified water.

Chad: We can arrange for your filters to be automatically shipped to you every 3, 6, or 12 months. Not only you will get free shipping on this order today, but also on every future water filter shipment. May I enroll you in our re-order program today?

Me: Because of my religious beliefs, I would have to find someone who is not Amish to change the filter and I don't know anyone who isn't. The guy two houses down the block from me never wears black clothes, mostly Hawaiian shirts, but he has a long beard and drinks like a fish so I'm not sure whether he's Amish or not.

Chad: John, would you like to enroll with the re-order program?

Me: No, Chad.

Chad: The filter can be re-ordered every three, six or twelve months! Each time the filter is re-ordered there is no shipping cost for filters.

Chad: There is no extra cost for this program and you'll only be charged for the water filter's price.

Chad: Is there any concern that you are not willing to enroll to this program?

Me: Chad are you with the Mafia or the Costa Nostra assuming they are two separate organizations? I'm really starting to feel intimidated a bit and don't want the filters but you're really making me get nervous. Is it ok if I say no to the filters? Do I have your word that you will you send thugs to my home or be angry with me and not allow me to purchase the gasket I need so desperately for my refrigerator?

Chad: No problem at all, please keep this offer in mind for future.

Chad: John, may I have your complete card number along with the expiration date, please? (I gave him the info)

Chad: Thank you for the card details.

Chad: Before I place your order, I am required to read the following disclosures to you.

Me: You're welcome, Chad.

101

Chad: John, to ensure that you receive your part order in a timely manner, this order is immediately processed. Once processed, this transaction cannot be changed or cancelled. You may return an unused and uninstalled part in its original packaging. Before you return your part, contact us or visit our website at www.SearsPartsDirect.com to obtain a Return Authorization number, which must be included with the returned part. We must receive the returned part(s) with the Return Authorization number within 90 days of your original order date. Credit will be issued for the part(s) and tax minus any shipping charges. You will receive an order confirmation for this order. This is not a bill, but a receipt confirming the order we are placing today.

Chad: The gasket, is a manufacturer authorized substitution, and may differ slightly in appearance from the original.

Chad: John, we will provide your order confirmation and order status updates through email. What is your email address?

Me: *(gave Chad my email address)*

Chad: Thank you.

Chad: Let me quickly summarize your order.

Chad: Your complete order total with shipping and tax is $60.62 and the order consists of door gasket and the estimated arrival date for your order is Sep 22

Chad: Let me submit the order and help you with the order number.

Me: Thank you.

Chad: You're welcome

Chad: Congratulations! The order number for your order is C358425.

Chad: You can check the order status any time at ww.searspartsdirect.com .

Me: Great, thanks, Chad! I appreciate all your help.

Chad: John, as a homeowner you are entitled to a free consultation on heating & cooling, windows & door, siding, kitchen re-modeling and cabinet refacing.

Chad: Thank you very mush.

Chad: *much

Chad: Our design consultant will contact you within 24-48 hours and tell you more about this.

Chad: Which are you interested in today and what would be the best time to contact you, would it be in the morning or evening?

Me: You're welcome. Oh, what was that deal again with the filters? My wife might be able to put them in. She's agnostic.

Chad: It is the promotional offer we have which could help you save shipping charges for today's order and as well as for the future filter re-orders.

Me: Oh, right. No, I'm good, Chad! I still don't want the filters but should I ever change my mind in the middle of the night, you'll be the first one I call. Thanks and have a nice weekend.

Chad: You're most welcome.

Chad: It was great chatting with you and helping you place this order.

Chad: Thank you for chatting with me; it was my pleasure to assist you. Thank you for choosing Sears Parts Directs today; we appreciate your business. Good bye! Have a happy week end!

Chat session has been terminated by the site operator.

Well, that's it. The whole transcript. By the time I got off the chat with Chad I could have knitted a refrigerator seal but you know, now that I have time to reflect on the experience, I feel we made a connection today, Chad and I. Two men out there in cyberspace keeping the whole big world economy spinning along, one refrigerator gasket replacement order at a time. Or 30 minutes, whichever comes first.

HOW TO PROLONG YOUR LIFE

Since the dawn of Time when apes began walking on the planet, to the late morning, perhaps early afternoon of Time when they evolved into human beings, Man has been trying to attain immortality — a state which could mean eternal life for some, or for most, living long enough to sell your house for $150 more than what you paid for it.

Today in 2011, people dream of living longer, extending their lives through proper nutrition, meditation and exercise so that they may not only be around to enjoy watching their grandchildren and their grandchildren's children play outside their nursing home window, but to enjoy playing right alongside them, even competing against them in full contact sports such as rugby, lacrosse and cage fighting.Is this a realistic expectation?

Can people really control how long they live? Can a 103 year old woman execute a half guard escape to single leg and then use a hip over sweep to immobilize her 23 year old, 178 pound grandson to win the Ultimate Fighting Championship? Well, for the last question, the answer is probably yes, because I heard those cage fighting things are fixed but as far as putting death on permanent hiatus?

The answer, sadly is no. Nobody lives forever. That is a fact of life. No one, except perhaps Mickey Rooney, an actor of such diminutive stature it's rumored that he's not even on God's or the Devil's radar screen, but Mr. Rooney aside, there are techniques all of us can employ to prolong life, or to at least make life appear longer than it actually is. And isn't that enough?

Good! I heard someone say, "Yes".

10 Simple Things You Can Do To Make Your Life Seem Longer

1. Drink 24, 8 ounce glasses of water every 15 minutes

2. Call your insurance agent and tell him you need "the works".

3. Adapt the batter box component of professional baseball for business. During every meeting you attend, raise your hand to get the attention of your boss while simultaneously standing up and walking several feet away from your chair. Take several long moments to adjust your tie, extend the cuffs of your shirt from your suit jacket, tap the bottom of your shoes with your briefcase or one belonging to a coworker or customer and after raising your hand once again to signal the attention of your boss that you are ready to return to your seat, return to your seat. Repeat this exercise as much as possible as it will also help to make life seem longer for everyone else in the conference room.

4. Tivo the US Farm Report and watch the week's episodes in one sitting. To further enhance the illusion of time standing still, transcribe each episode using a calligraphy pen.

5. If you are married and male, let your wife pick the movie on date night. If you are married and female, savor every moment of the movie you picked on date night.

6. After ordering, wait for your breakfast to arrive at a Cracker Barrel restaurant.

7. Spend a day in Pennsylvania.

8. Try to get a child who is sobbing uncontrollably to tell you what happened.

9. Watch anything with Renee Zellweger in it.

10. Go #2 in a Porta Potty.

I hope that these suggestions help you to better manage the passing of time and give you a sense of being able to control the velocity of each passing moment. The whole thing's an illusion of course but what do you want from me? Anybody can start a blog. I didn't even have to give them my real name.

WHAT'S WITH ALL THE CHATTER?

I don't know why the government and the media used the word "chatter" to describe the back and forth communication of evil plotting by terrorist organizations. Chatter just seems synonymous with "gossip" and every time I hear it I picture intelligence experts listening intently to a bunch of guys shooting the bull like a couple of those cartoon chipmunks in the old Warner Brothers cartoons.

Terrorist #1: "You'll never guess what 'Mr. You'll Never Catch Me Coming Out of the Hideout' expects us to do at the German Embassy."

Terrorist #2: "Don't get me started with that guy. John Wayne in short pants."

Terrorist #1: "And how about dinner last night? Sixty of us and he sends out for 60 White Castle hamburgers. You got to be kidding me. I could eat 60 of those myself! They're what? Thirty-cents a piece? Cheap son of a…and did you see him trying to look tough holding the AK47 at the photo shoot? Benzi started laughing and had to run out of the cave."

Terrorist #2: "My Labradoodle's more intimidating than him. You gonna finish that scone? What is it, blueberry?"

Terrorist #1: "Yeah, take it. I'm carbed out."

Terrorist #2: "Thanks. Getting back to reality for a minute. You have a decent auto mechanic? I need one that's not a crook. The timing belt is going on the Opel and you get a thief, they'll charge you a grand easy."

Terrorist #1: "You want my opinion, I wouldn't sink another nickel into the junk box. You should lease something. Uh oh. The big cheese just pulled up.   Better pick up those hamburger wrappers."

Terrorist #2: "How does he look? Does he look mad?

Terrorist #1: Hard to tell. (sounds of boots stomping and heavy breathing)

Terrorists #1 and #2: Greetings Oh Great One. How are things at the command center?

Oh Great One: How should I know? I was at the chiropractor's all morning. Any scones left?

TOP TEN TIPS FOR THANKSGIVING TURKEYS

As much as I enjoy eating roasted turkey on Thanksgiving, and turkey sandwiches the day after Thanksgiving and then nothing turkey related after that for at least six to ten months, I have always felt guilty about the vast number of these creatures who, thanklessly, are forced to give up their lives for this national holiday in order for us to feel thankful about ours, and in no small part because we're having roast turkey and all the trimmings for supper! My wife makes a sausage stuffing that... well, I'm digressing a bit here so we'll save that discussion for another time.

Anyway, after hearing about the turkey who actually refused to accept a Presidential Thanksgiving pardon which would have spared his life, arguing eloquently and passionately that the New York Jets needed a pardon more than he did, I decided that I could no longer stand on the sidelines. So, two days after Thanksgiving, while having a steaming bowl of soup — tomato bisque if you're wondering, wise guy1 — I came up with a ten-step survival guide to give turkeys a fighting chance. So without further adieu...

Ten Tips to Help Turkeys Avoid Becoming Thanksgiving Turkeys

1. If you hear a loud bang in the woods, let someone else "see what all the excitement's about".

2. Avoid all social events and informal get togethers during hunting season, but always send regrets so other turkeys don't think badly of you.

3. If you can afford a vacation and still have days left in November, Portland, OR has the largest vegan population in the United States.

4. If you live on a turkey farm, never be first in line for anything.

5. Remember, hanging out with a deer during hunting season is like getting a ride home from Lindsay Lohan at two in the morning.

6. The secret that you can only fly for around 15 feet or so is out.

7. Since you really can't fly, don't walk around with other turkeys in a V formation. This has nothing to do with self preservation. It just looks silly.

8. Hunters often use turkey calls to lure you within shooting range so if you hear someone say something about you that seems just too flattering to be true, it probably is. Don't respond.

9. Contrary to popular belief, the odds of your being the turkey who gets pardoned by the President of the United States is not directly proportionate to the amount of money you've donated to the Democratic party.

10. Never stick your neck out for anyone.

FATHER'S DAY

This weekend marks another Father's Day and while I'm not fond of holidays that have been kidnapped and raised by Madison Avenue executives -- I am very fond of my father --and therefore grudgingly indebted to the advertising industry for providing this opportunity to tell you why.

First off, I've known the man for years. He was there the day I was born and was at my house last night at 9:30 when he dropped off my three-year old daughter who has a little difficulty honoring sleep over commitments she makes herself. There has never been a time when my father has not been in my life, even when I lived three thousand miles away.

Growing up, our family was not what you would call an "I love you" family. We didn't say "I love you" before we went off to work or school or to get something out of the basement and we didn't have any Walton nighttime rituals ending with one note harmonica solos. There's nothing wrong with that of course, it just wasn't our thing.

My father's expressions of love came from what he did, not what he said. When we were little he took my brothers and me with him everywhere he could. We went to the beach, the park, the drive-in, we drove to Florida. When we played ball in the street, he played too.

Even as a surly, often unpleasant teenager, I knew my father loved me. I used to come in through the front door some nights and like Kato and the

Green Hornet, he would launch a sneak attack, leaping out from behind a sofa and wrestling me to the ground -- eliciting a laugh from both of us and allowing me to forget my role, at least temporarily as an adolescent malcontent.

Of all the things my father has provided my brothers and I over the years, the things I value most outside of his willingness to help me keep my house from falling apart, is his sense of fair play and his sense of humor.

I have never met a more consistently decent man in my life, one whose moral and ethical compass always points to true north. I've been next to him when he stopped his car on the side of the road to help a woman change a tire. I've seen him offer lifts to people caught in the rain and shovel snow as if he didn't know where his sidewalks began and his neighbor's ended. His loyalty and compassion to friends and family, particularly those who are in poor health, is beyond words. I have never known him to harbor a grudge.

While I come from a family with a great sense of humor, there are members who are "joke funny" and those who are naturally funny – meaning the humor comes from what's going on the moment-- not from reciting a joke. My father is of the latter category and on the right day could make Queen Elizabeth snort milk through her nose during a funeral.

I was standing next to him one day when the phone rang and a salesman tried to get my parents to come to the Poconos for a free weekend in exchange for listening to a timeshare pitch. After three minutes my father finally got his chance to speak. "This sounds terrific," he said. "I could really use a vacation after the year I had. They just repossessed my car but if you can send someone to pick us up and drive us down -- we're in!" The salesman hung up.

One of the best decisions I have ever made was to move back to the town I grew up in after being away in California for 14 years. After my wife and I had our first two children, palm trees, the ocean, warm weather, earthquakes, riots, fires and mudslides just lost their allure when we realized what our children were missing due to only seeing their grandparents two or three times a year.

We moved to New Jersey in 1997 and I've never regretted the decision once. My wife on the other hand is from New Orleans, as is most her family, and while her perception of our decision and living in New Jersey may vary somewhat from mine, her unbridled passion for Taylor Ham, a delicacy not found south of Delaware, has bound her to the Garden State for now and forever or until such a time as it finds it way to Louisiana.

My father and I play tennis together almost every week and we generally see each other every day. I will admit his frequent visits to our house have more to do with seeing or picking up our youngest daughter. She and my father are inseparable and the joy they exude being in each other's company is contagious.

I can't subscribe to the notion that familiarity breeds contempt because when I consider the time I've spent with my father over the years, I know that familiarity breeds respect. He's a great friend and an inspiration and if I were a sentimental type, I'd tell him that I love him -- but more than likely when he comes in with my daughter from the beach this afternoon -- I'll probably just sneak up from behind and tackle him to the floor.

*****

ABOUT THE AUTHOR

John Hartnett has worked in the restaurant, construction, entertainment, greeting card and publishing industries, among others -- and once had a job in California selling investments in gas wells over the phone but was fired after his boss overheard him quietly pleading with potential clients to hang up on him. He lives with his wife and three children in New Jersey. The Barber's Conundrum is his second book.

16364663R00070

Made in the USA
Charleston, SC
16 December 2012